the art of
Support

Reaching Out to Others
in Times of Loss

BY LEE FRANKLIN

GIFT BOOKS
from Hallmark

table of *Contents*

Published by Hallmark Books,
a division of Hallmark Cards, Inc.,
Kansas City, MO 64108
Visit us on the Web
at www.Hallmark.com.

Editorial Director: Todd Hafer
Editor: Jeff Morgan
Art Director: Kevin Swanson
Design: Mary Eakin, Alison Bauer
Illustration: David Pjecha, Mary Eakin
Production Artist: Dan Horton

ISBN: 978-1-59530-187-1
BOK4333
Printed and bound in China

Introduction

Is it me, or is life today getting harder?
It seems that in the last few years, my circle
of family, friends, co-workers, and neighbors
has gone through so much. A friend
recently called to say her biopsy results
were not good. Just this morning, a co-worker
told me that she had to put Thistle, her
beloved Scottish terrier, to sleep. My
neighbor's brother was recently in a severe
car accident. What can I possibly say
to provide support to these people who
so badly need it? What can I do? So often,
I feel completely inadequate to respond
to the situation at hand. Where's the *Life
101* book when I need it?

When we don't know what to say or do, we often
do nothing—just to avoid saying or doing the wrong thing.
That used to be my tendency—before I started doing research
for this book. I was at the gym a while back and saw Al,
a man whom I used to work with at Hallmark. I immediately
remembered that he had tragically lost his wife about a year
ago. Because I didn't know him well and probably because
I never know if I should go to funerals or not, I didn't go
to the services. I didn't send a card. I know I should have
(especially since I'm a card writer!), but I didn't.

So there I was, on the triceps machine, when I spotted
him from the corner of my eye. (Beating myself up for my
lack of social graces was more painful than the weights
at that moment.) My first inclination was to avoid him—
to avoid facing my own social ineptness and my regret
at not having been more responsive when his wife died.
But because I was in the process of writing this book, I
would not let myself off the hook. I knew from my research
that it is a good thing to reach out to others in times of loss,
even when it feels uncomfortable to do so.

And so I did what this book will elaborate: I initiated
contact. I was real. To begin, I said little more than "I'm
so sorry." I listened carefully to anything he wanted to
say, and I expressed my deep sympathy. I told him what
I remembered about his wife from the few times I had met
her—that she had a vibrancy about her that lit up the room,
that she was supersmart and deeply compassionate—

all traits that I thought must have served her well in her counseling profession. He smiled as I was talking and echoed my thoughts, telling me how her clients deeply missed her. I told him how I loved seeing the two of them together—how they had seemed so happy. It was a second marriage for both, and he talked about his gratitude that they had had twelve incredible years together. He went on to tell me about how they were in the process of remodeling their home when she died. He talked about the challenge of living out their dream without her presence. I asked how he was doing at meeting this challenge, and he said, "Depends on the day." I ended by again saying, "I'm so sorry."

The whole exchange took less than ten minutes, but at the end of it, we both had tears in our eyes. I truly felt the weight of his pain—even 1 year 3 months and 17 days after his wife's death (his response to my question of when). My heart truly went out to him, and I think he felt that. For those ten minutes, the memory of his wife and all she meant to him and to so many others burned brightly in our little corner of the weight room. Al carries her memory with him every minute of every day. But for these minutes, he shared it with someone who truly cared, and he seemed grateful.

I offer this account to demonstrate that reaching out to others in times of loss is easier than one might think and more rewarding than one might imagine. Knowing a few basics about helpful ways to reach out makes the process rewarding for both the one going through the loss and for the one providing support.

This book is written to share insights about loss and grief and to offer simple and genuine ways to appropriately respond to those who are grieving any kind of loss.

Hallmark exists to enrich lives by helping people to connect. Even I, as a Hallmark writer who deals with personal communication professionally, know how hard it can be to connect and be supportive during times of loss (as my initial AI avoidance response indicates). Hallmark believes that it is important to connect in all times of life, especially in difficult times when others truly need support. We are committed to giving our customers everything they need to connect with others—and hence the idea for this book.

a qualifier: Throughout this book, I suggest that those supporting people who are grieving do so by sending cards. This may seem to be self-serving, for Hallmark's benefit. I continually make the suggestion, because greeting cards are a wonderful way for supporters to express ongoing care to those who are grieving. In fact, personal handwritten notes on stationery are fine, too. Cards and notes, more than e-mail, show that the supporter took time and effort to express care and concern. They can be sent throughout the grieving process. And most important, cards and notes can be engaged on the griever's terms, on the griever's timetable. And they can be saved as reminders that the griever is not alone.

In preparing to write about this subject, I have done extensive research on loss, grief, and ways to be supportive to those who are grieving. As part of my research, many in the Hallmark community have shared with me their stories of loss and have offered suggestions for providing support to others based on their own experiences.

I will mention and repeat again and again that every person's journey of grief is individual. No two people respond to loss in the same way. There is no one timetable for grief, nor is there one *right* way to deal with loss. In the same way, there is no one way to provide support. The support that is offered depends on the relationship between the supporter and the griever, the personalities involved, the physical proximity of the people involved, and many other factors. Though there is not one right way to grieve or to provide support, there are guidelines and principles that can facilitate the grieving process.

This book has been written in hopes of being as user-friendly as possible to those supporting the grieving. Because supporters can be more helpful to those grieving if they have a basic understanding of loss, grief, and support, the first three chapters offer an introduction to these topics. Chapter 1 discusses aspects of loss, Chapter 2 discusses grief—the natural response to loss, and Chapter 3 presents general ways to be supportive to those who are grieving. Chapter 4 features a practical "To-Be List" of ways to be supportive in and through all kinds of loss. Chapters 5-9 address specific kinds of loss and, for each case, suggest specific means of being supportive to augment the list in Chapter 4. These chapters include accounts from real people who have experienced these losses. Chapter 10, "On a Supportive Note," then gives examples of notes that can be written and sent to those who have experienced various kinds of loss.

This book does not directly address specific ways to support children in their journeys of grief. Supporting children through grief requires particular sensitivities and approaches that are beyond the scope of this book. Resources for doing so are provided in the appendix.

I suggest that in reading this book, you begin with the first three chapters, then use the rest of the book on an as-needed basis. Of course, if you have immediate need to respond to a loss situation, you may want to scan the "To-Be List" to find ways of offering support that best fit the situation, your personality, and your relationship with the griever. You can then turn to the chapter that most fits the kind of loss to find additional ways to offer support for that specific situation. However you use this book, I hope that it helps you to more confidently reach out to others in their times of loss.

chapter one

understanding
Loss

My Interest in Loss

When my 20-year marriage was coming
to an end, I expected to feel sad, depressed,
overwhelmed. But there were so many
things that I didn't expect and couldn't
understand. Why was I so tired? Why was
I having such trouble concentrating? Why
did I keep locking my keys in my car? Why
was I getting in so many accidents? (I crashed
my car twice in six months.) I knew I wasn't
functioning at a very high capacity.

I had read somewhere that it helps to set goals. So my daily to-do list looked something like this:

✓ **Get out of bed in the morning.**

✓ **Once I get out of bed, do not get back in bed.**

✓ **Do not lock my keys in the car.**

✓ **Do not hit any cars.**

Some days I met my goals. Some days I didn't. Looking back, it's hard to remember being in such a desperate place, but at the time, just getting through the day was a major challenge.

If I had known more about loss and grief, I would have felt less crazy in the process. Of course, I'm not the only one to experience loss. Everywhere I look, it seems people I know are going through times of loss. There is the major type of loss—death. But there are so many other losses— divorce, breakup with a longtime romantic partner, job loss or demotion, retirement and the losses of social interaction and role definition that a life change like it can bring, loss of health or mobility, property loss due to theft or disaster, and financial loss. The list goes on and on. As our friends and families face these situations, we long to be supportive and helpful. To effectively provide support for those who are enduring the effects of loss, it helps to know some basics about loss.

loss lesson #1: *Loss Happens*

It happens to all of us throughout life. Accepting this basic fact is helpful in understanding loss and knowing how to respond to it. For instance, there is a tendency when we hear about loss to try to find some reason why it happened. A friend is diagnosed with lung cancer. "Did he smoke?" is our first question. We hear of someone who had a stroke. "How old was she?" we ask, hoping the answer is "way, way older than you." We ask these questions because we want to make sense of loss. We want to establish a causal relationship that distances us from the loss: this awful thing happened because he/she did something that my loved ones and I wouldn't do or now we know not to do. We think that if we can establish cause and effect, then we can make sense of something that often defies reason. If we can explain away the loss, then we can feel that we have more control and that we can protect our loved ones and ourselves from loss.

It is a fallacy to think that we can avoid loss. Loss happens. To effectively support others, it is necessary to deal with our own fears, anxieties, and insecurities about loss. When we realize this most basic fact of life—that loss happens— the tendency to say unhelpful things is lessened.

Understanding that loss is inevitable takes us away from critical or distancing behaviors that ever so subtly place blame on the victims. "He had a terrible diet. No wonder he had a heart attack." "She shouldn't have been driving so late at night. No wonder she was in an accident." When we suggest blame for the loss, we echo the griever's worst fear—that there could have been something to prevent the loss. Grievers do not need or want someone reminding them of what could have been done differently. Regret is not especially helpful in the grieving process. When we accept that loss happens, we can offer support without adding guilt or blame.

When my mom's friend, Marilyn, told friends the troubling news that her husband's MRI revealed three suspicious-looking spots on his lung, one friend said that it was too bad Jack had been a smoker for so long. This friend was, in all likelihood, understandably trying to reassure herself that she and her loved ones were safe from such a scary diagnosis, but blurting out something like that is not helpful to some-one who needs support now more than ever. Believe me, Marilyn has not forgotten for one second that her husband has smoked for more than 40 years. Supporters who feel they can point to a cause can feel insulated from the danger of loss if they or their loved ones are not at risk.

The danger that comes from thinking that we can avoid loss is twofold. First, to think we can avoid loss can inhibit us from acknowledging and dealing with the losses that naturally occur throughout the course of life. I'm talking here not only about the big losses, like death, but also the seemingly small losses, like the loss an elderly person experiences when he can no longer drive, the theft of a piece of heirloom jewelry, the death of a relationship. The second danger is that it distances us from victims of loss at a time when they need our support and understanding the most. People going through loss can interpret such questions as judgments and reproaches, an interpretation that can cause them to feel even worse, which is definitely not our intent as supporters.

Loss happens. Loss is part of life. When we accept that, we can use the energy that we would spend hoping that it doesn't happen to us to deal with our own losses and be present in a supportive and nonjudgmental way to others experiencing loss who desperately need support.

loss lesson #2: *There Are Many "Little Deaths" in Life*

In our culture, death is the form of loss that receives the most attention, and for good reason. Death is profound in its life-altering effects on those who must face this world without the presence and companionship of a loved one.

There are many cultural practices and rituals in place to help those grieving a death. The funeral, the eulogy, the burial, the after-funeral dinner, the sympathy cards— all are traditional practices to let the grieving know that they are surrounded by love and care during a difficult time.

But there are other losses that are also profound in their effects, for which there are no established grieving practices. These losses can be just as life-altering. For instance, when a person divorces, loses a job, experiences diminished physical or mental capacity because of health-related issues, or suffers the loss of important material possessions, there is often significant reason to grieve. The victim must go on with life, though life has been significantly altered by an event which we might characterize as a "little death."

Supporters can help those who have experienced little deaths by listening attentively to what their losses mean to them.

There is a tendency to minimize little losses, even by those going through the loss. They may think that because the loss is not death or because it is not life-threatening that there is no true reason to grieve. If the person suffering the loss can truly acknowledge the loss and allow himself or herself to grieve the loss, restored wholeness can come sooner.

There is also a tendency for supporters to minimize the loss caused by little deaths if they do not grasp the magnitude of the loss. One way of minimizing is by trying to point out to the griever how the situation could have been worse. They may do so by one-upping the story. When a woman finds out she needs a mastectomy, the one listening quickly jumps in to tell about another woman who had a double mastectomy and didn't have insurance. In an instant, the attention and focus is off the woman who has just learned the devastating news that she will lose an important part of her physical self. The supporter has not heard the woman's feelings about her significant loss. Even if the intent is to offer reassurance by pointing to others who have survived worse, the supporter is not being helpful to the griever by one-upping the loss. When a supporter listens empathetically to the griever and does not minimize the loss, grieving is facilitated.

Another way others minimize the loss of little deaths is by trying to get the griever to look on the bright side. When a teenager totals the used Camaro he bought with his life's savings, a natural response is, "At least you weren't hurt. That would have been so much worse." That is absolutely true, but at that moment, the teen feels it is the absolute worst. His world has been significantly changed—and not for the better. He's lost his independence, his prized possession, the reason he sacked groceries for two full summers. He's lost his feeling of invincibleness. And if he gets a response like that, he's lost the opportunity to share his grief with someone who can create the space to receive what he wants to share because the "supporter" has already told him how he should feel. The griever can even feel guilty in the face of such a dismissive response in that he should feel grateful, but he doesn't. Supporters can help those who have experienced little deaths by hearing what their losses mean and by being present for them in their time of grief.

The grieving process for these situations can be very similar to that of death. A loss of a significant person, role, or thing can cause the death of dreams, the death of a way of life, the death of an expected future. Supporters can help victims by allowing them to talk about their feelings of loss caused by little deaths. Ways of supporting the grieving will be offered in Chapter 3, with more specific suggestions offered in Chapters 4-9.

loss lesson #3: looking at loss
From Both Sides Now

Another dimension of loss concerns the roles of people affected by the loss. In some types of loss, there can be a tendency, consciously or subconsciously, for observers to see the loss in terms of the one who initiated it and the one who is victim. When we hear of a divorce, often we ask, "Who filed?" We may assume that the one who initiates the separation will have an easier time dealing with the loss than the one being left. When high school grads leave home either for college or to start their lives on their own, we often assume that those choosing to leave will have an easier time with the change than the family members left behind.

The point is that unless loss is caused by death, accident, or disaster, loss is usually not one-sided. There are obvious effects experienced by loss "victims." But "initiators" often experience effects, too—such as guilt, doubt, regret, or remorse. Loss is never easy. It's always complex and multi-faceted, impacting everyone involved in different ways. Realizing this can help one be supportive to those who leave and also to those being left.

loss lesson #4:
the Limitations of Loss Support

Someone who wants to support a person who is grieving can most effectively help by realizing this loss lesson: *There is a limit to what you can do.* Equally important: *Though a supporter's role is limited, it is crucial.*

I offer this paradoxical loss lesson because it is helpful for a supporter to go into this tender space of human care with realistic expectations. When a person has experienced profound loss, nothing a supporter can say will make it better. Nothing a supporter can do will take away the pain. There is nothing anyone can do to hasten the individual grief journey that each grieving person must walk.

The limited effects of support can be frustrating to accept. We long to take away our loved ones' pain. We wish there were more we could do. By not understanding the limitations of our supportive roles, though, we may add to the griever's pain. A young widow whose 33-year-old husband died told me how it hurt to see her mother and sister hurting so much for her. The widow wished she could feel better—not so much for her own sake, but for the sake of her mother and sister. But she couldn't fake healing. She felt guilty when their blatant attempts to help did not achieve the lifted spirits they desired. *A supporter's role is not to take away the pain; a supporter's role is to accompany the griever in and through the pain.*

All of this is not to diminish the benefits of support for one moment. Support is crucial for one who has experienced loss. Being present to people in their pain can help them feel validated, understood, and supported all along their own personal journeys of grief. It's hard to believe that a supporter's silent presence can make a difference to a person who is too grief-stricken to speak. But it can. It's hard to believe that a response of "I'm so sorry" or "I hear you" can be helpful. But it can. It's hard to believe that sending flowers or cards in the weeks and months after the loss can be life-giving. But it can.

When various people offer support in ways that are appropriate to the relationship and responsive to the griever's needs, this support can facilitate the person's process of grief. In Chapter 3, we will focus on ways to be supportive to those grieving. But first, it is helpful to understand more about the grief process itself.

chapter two

understanding

Grief

Good Grief

Now that we've looked at loss, let's turn our attention to grief, which is the normal, natural response to loss. It is important to understand some basics about grief so that supporters can effectively accompany others along their journeys of grief. In this chapter, we'll delve a little bit deeper into grief and examine not only what it is but what it feels like to someone who is living with the effects of loss.

It is important to be reminded that every grief experience is individual. Grief is particular and unique to each person who has experienced a loss. The effects of grief will depend on the person's personality, the level of investment in what was lost, the person's age and support system, and other factors. But, though every experience of grief is individual, there are universal aspects of grief. Understanding these universals about grief can help supporters to be more understanding and knowledgeable companions to those along the grief journey. The journey takes as long as it takes. There's no hurrying the person along. But it can help to know the goal, the desired destination, of a productive grief process.

The goal of grief is to gradually detach enough from the loss so as to form new and life-giving attachments with other persons, situations, and things. By life-giving attachments, I mean commitments to people or situations that help one to engage in a life that has renewed meaning, challenge, vibrancy, balance, affection, and/or spirituality in the shadow of loss. (Examples of unhealthy attachments would be attaching to people, situations, or substances for the purpose of becoming numb to life so as to dull the pain.) Getting to this destination is not easy. It is a journey that every person must take, in large part, by himself, though companions who accompany the griever can make the rough spots smoother and give assurance that the griever will undoubtedly come out on the other side.

What Grief Feels Like:

As I mentioned earlier, when I was going through my divorce after a 20-year marriage, I kept locking my keys in my car. I had the number to my roadside auto service on speed dial. I just couldn't seem to remember to take my keys out of my car before I locked the door. I lost other things, too. I would search and search for my wallet and finally find it in the refrigerator. I couldn't remember how to get to the baseball field where my son regularly had practice. Not only had I lost my marriage, I thought, I was losing my mind! Had I known more about the effects of grief, I would have had more patience with myself.

There are many ways to feel the effects of grief, with seven that are most universal. I call them the Seven Dwarfs of Despair. These are the little guys you wouldn't want to in-vite to your next party. But these are the fellows that moved in and became my roommates for quite some time. Had I known they were coming, I might have been a little more understanding of their wily ways and irritating habits. For those supporting the grieving, it is helpful to be able to recognize these unwanted guests, who are often the first to show up and the last to leave after a loss.

The Seven Dwarfs of Despair

#1: *Spacey*

It is quite normal in the grieving process for the griever to become distracted, disoriented, and numb—all characteristics of Spacey, the first dwarf to show up after a loss. When Spacey moves in, things can become confusing. Objects can start disappearing. It can become hard to concentrate. And don't let Spacey in the car, because he has no sense of direction or focus.

Though Spacey can make life frustrating, he means well. When someone experiences profound loss, the physical, mental, and spiritual body undergoes a state of shock. The body protects itself by entering a temporary state of numbness. At the same time, the mind is working overtime to convince the rest of the body that the loss has not really occurred or that it is not so severe. It is in this phase that denial can set in. The body is confused. It's like all these alarms have gone off in the body—some are saying "TAKE COVER!" Others are saying "False Alarm." Still others are saying "System Overload—need to shut down and eventually reboot." No wonder disorientation happens.

Spacey can make himself at home for a good (or not so good) long time. The good thing is that this is the mind's way of protecting the body from being overwhelmed with feelings. The bad thing is that if people do not understand this part of the grief process, they can feel frustrated with themselves at best and crazy at worst. In his book *A Grief Observed,* C. S. Lewis writes about his grief experience after the death of his beloved wife: "At times it feels like being mildly drunk, or concussed. There is a sort of invisible blanket between the world and me. I find it hard to take in what anyone says. Or perhaps, hard to want to take it in. It is so uninteresting. Yet I want the others to be about me. I dread the moments when the house is empty. If only they would talk to one another, not to me."

Supporters can help the griever by recognizing Spacey's influence and by responding in appropriate ways. Offering reassurance to the griever that numbness, confusion, and disorientation are normal (and temporary) parts of the grieving process can be extremely helpful.

There can be other practical ways to help as well. A supporter who is helping from afar can listen empathetically by phone. If it is appropriate, the supporter can offer to help prioritize tasks and/or offer assistance with those that require focus and concentration. Supporters in close proximity may help by arranging transportation to appointments and by taking notes in meetings with lawyers, insurance agents, or doctors. When supporters pay attention to the griever's needs and capabilities and offer specific ways to be helpful, Spacey can have a short, harmless stay.

#2 & #3: *Empty & Lonely*

When Spacey leaves, other dwarfs tend to move in—particularly Empty and his cohort Lonely. The two are a lot alike, but once a griever has lived with them a while, the subtle differences become more apparent. Lonely is more outgoing—more of an external focus. Lonely reminds grievers that their world is minus a very, very significant person or situation or thing. Lonely sidles right up next to the griever, making himself at home, constantly reminding the griever that things are never going to be the same.

Empty is more introverted—focused on the pain within. Emptiness is the feeling of nothingness inside. When I was grieving my marriage, I remember feeling like a big meringue cookie. I had a hard exterior shell, but it could so easily be cracked, and inside was nothing but empty air. I just couldn't figure out why all this emptiness hurt so much.

Joan Didion, in her profound and honest account of the year after her husband's death, *The Year of Magical Thinking,* writes of her experience with emptiness. In discussing grief, she says that before it is experienced, it is impossible to know "the unending absence that follows, the void, the very opposite of meaning, the relentless succession of moments during which we will confront the experience of meaninglessness itself."

The reason Empty and Lonely become so quickly at home with the grieving is because there is such a huge vacancy. When a person invests himself or herself in people, situations, and things, these become a part of the person. "She was my better half," the grieving widower says. "I'm my son's mom—it's my reason for being," says a stay-at-home mom. "Baseball is my life," says the teenage boy. When the people, situation, or things are lost, the griever loses a significant part of himself or herself. The long road of grief involves the person reengaging life in a way that no longer includes the person, situation, or thing that has been lost.

Remember *Humpty Dumpty*? After his fall, "All the king's horses and all the king's men couldn't put Humpty together again." The goal of grief is for the griever to be able to once again be "together"—even though a significant piece is missing. The thing for supporters to remember is that though the piece is gone, it is present in a different way—in the form of memory. Supporters can help put the griever's life back together again by helping to establish the missing piece in the memory category. Supporters can do so by asking about the loss, listening to stories, seeing pictures, helping to make a memory book—anything that helps to establish the missing piece as a memory. As the griever realizes that the missing piece is not missing in entirety, but that what was lost still exists as a memory, loneliness and emptiness can be lessened.

Supporters can accompany the grieving as they attempt to put the pieces of their lives back together. The process is slow and can't be rushed. But by accompanying the griever along the road of grief, the companionship can help keep

Empty and Lonely from taking over. More specific examples of ways to be supportive will be offered in Chapters 3-9.

#4: *Guilty*

When the dwarf Guilty moves in, there's constant chatter. Most of Guilty's sentences begin with "You should have…" or "Why didn't you…" or "Why aren't you…" Guilty hasn't accepted Loss Lesson #1—that *Loss Happens.* So he's looking for someone to blame. Or at least he's looking for a way that this loss could have been prevented. Guilty feels that if he can say that he was the bad guy, then the loss was not random. He has control over the situation, because he can believe (in his distorted thinking) that the loss was all his fault. But this sense of control comes at a cost—the cost of self-blame, which is not at all helpful in the grieving process.

Grievers can feel guilt in the face of loss for several reasons— and these reasons don't have to be rational. The rational dwarf is usually a no-show in times of loss. One reason grievers feel guilt is because they feel that they contributed to the cause of the loss. In matters of death, many feel there was more they could or should have done. In relational loss, such as a divorce or breakup, grievers can often dwell on their faults and failings—forgetting that it takes two to make a relationship thrive or fail. In loss of property, grievers can flail themselves for a careless or thoughtless act that put their property in jeopardy or they can chastise themselves for things they neglected to do to avoid the loss. Supporters can help grievers by reminding them that loss happens. Supporters also can help by offering compassion and by reminding that we are put on this earth to be human, not to be perfect. When supporters help kick Guilty to the curb, Mercy can more quickly take up permanent residence.

Secondly, grievers can feel guilty for the way they are handling their grief. Guilty says "You should be over this by now" or "You're acting irrational" or "You should be handling this better than you are." Grief truly alters one's way of being, and it is not an easy adjustment for people to make. By assuring grievers that the grief process is normal and necessary, support- ers facilitate good grieving. Through their receptive responses that allow any and all expressions of emotion (including the griever's silence), supporters can show that the griever's way of grieving is exactly what he or she should be doing.

A third reason grievers can feel guilty is for the effect the griever's pain is having on the supporters. Guilty says, "I'm sorry to be such a downer" and "I'm terrible company" and "Don't feel you have to hang around me." There is

The best supporters allow grievers to let their true feelings show.

an underlying assumption that people only want to be in the company of those who are entertaining and uplifting. Supporters can help grievers by creating a safe, open emotional space for the grievers to be in, whatever mood they are in (tearful, happy, quiet), as they travel the precarious emotional road of grief.

The best supporters are the kinds of people who allow the grievers to let their true feelings show. If the griever is feeling sad, angry, or uncommunicative, a supporter can offer a silent, supportive presence. Recall one of the Loss Lessons— The Limitations of Loss Support. Support is not intended to take away pain or fix the situation. Supporters help most by appropriately accompanying the person in and through the pain. That way, if at the end of the phone or physical visit the griever does not seem cheered up, the supporter does not have to feel that he or she has failed. Quite the contrary. If the griever feels safe enough with a supporter to let honest emotions show, the supporter is most likely being very helpful in the grief journey. When the supporter is there (physically or by phone or e-mail) through good and not-so-good times, the Guilty dwarf quickly can feel out of place.

#5: Worry

When Worry moves in, there's plenty to do. There's fretting, dreading, doubting, obsessing, and worst-case-scenario-ing. With Worry, there's never a dull or dread-free moment. Just sensing this anxious creature sitting beside you, biting his nails, and wringing his hands is enough to make you wish for Spacey to make his mind-numbing return.

Worry is the outward manifestation of the internal feeling of fear. Loss can trigger fear. An underlying fear many carry throughout life is the fear of abandonment. This fear begins when helpless children fear that their parents will go away and never return. When someone faces significant loss, the fear of abandonment becomes reality. No matter how the loss occurred, the griever can feel abandoned by what was once an important part of life.

The loss of a person, situation, or important thing is significant in its effect. Life must be lived in the absence of what was once a joyful and important presence. In his book *A Grief Observed,* C. S. Lewis said, "No one ever told me that grief felt so like fear. I am not afraid, but the sensation is like being afraid. The same fluttering in the stomach, the same restlessness...I keep on swallowing."

There are specific reasons for the fear that grief triggers. It is a natural response to fear what is unfamiliar. It is natural to fear facing a future that often must be redefined in the face of the loss. The griever can fear that he or she lacks the abilities, skills, or resources to face a different or uncertain future in light of the loss. The comfort of the familiar has been taken away; worry about what will be has taken comfort's place.

As supporters of the grieving, we can help put Worry in its proper place. Yes, Worry has a right to be there. Worry in the face of sudden change is an appropriate response. Worry can motivate grievers into doing what needs to be done. But given too much power, he can be paralyzing. So as supporters of the griever, we can let Worry in the car. As a passenger. A not-too-vocal passenger. In the backseat— the "waaaaaaay back," as one of my sons would say when banishing the other to the farthest backseat of the minivan. But Worry never, ever gets to drive.

Not letting Worry take over is easy to say, but not always easy for the griever to do. Supporters can often help by being present to the griever—either in person or by phone, e-mail, or through correspondence. When the griever feels alone is when Worry can be exacerbated. The comforting presence of a caring supporter can do much to make the griever feel an increased sense of safety and security. With a caring supporter around, Worry has to work harder to get a foothold in the conversation.

#6: Angry

The Angry dwarf usually makes an appearance somewhere along the journey of grief. Anger is a common, though often misunderstood, component of grief. Anger happens for many reasons. When the griever is the one who was left (by death or through divorce or breakup), much anger can surface. The griever may be angry at having to go on with life in the absence of a significant partner. There may be financial or situational hardships that now must be faced alone. When a person loses a role that was important, there can be anger as well, especially when the loss was not by choice. Job loss, being cut from a sports team, a rejection from a desired college, a transfer to an undesired city—all can be infuriating to a person who would not choose this change. There can be anger over health challenges: A tennis player must give up her beloved game because of ongoing shoulder injuries; a senior citizen must give up the ability to drive when safety is at stake. There can be anger over material loss—a house fire destroys both memories and dreams; a financial loss significantly alters a standard of living. When someone loses an important person, situation, or thing and now must go on with life in the shadow of profound loss, it can be infuriating. In any circumstance, anger can be difficult to express—and to hear. We are not well-trained in our society to express or receive anger; often anger is avoided rather than effectively processed.

Typically in the face of loss, there are two responses to the Angry dwarf's presence—grievers either let him have the run of the house or they banish him to the basement and pretend he's not there. Both responses give Angry a lot of power.

When he's given the run of the house, ranting at anyone and everyone who will listen, it is easy to see how he has taken over—especially if no other emotions are allowed any space. Supporters can help by creating a safe emotional space to receive whatever the griever is feeling—even, and especially, anger. Unless the griever gets violent, the supporter need not fear authentic expressions of anger. The supporter can helpfully respond by hearing, acknowledging, and validating the anger, saying, "You sound very angry" or "Of course you're furious; this is terrible!" or "You have every right to be angry. It's normal to be angry in situations like this." When Angry is ruling the roost, such affirming, nondismissive comments can help to diffuse anger's complete power.

When Angry is banished to the basement, he has power as well. Though he may not always be seen, he can send his messages in subtle ways—through heating ducts and vents—so that the Angry fumes are everywhere. An example might be a woman who can't be mad at her husband dying—because that would be wrong or irrational. So she is mad at the nurses who did a lousy job of taking care of him, at the neighbors who were thoughtless, at the florist who sent inferior flowers. When anger goes underground, supporters who are close to the grievers may be able to let the griever know that it is okay to be angry at the person, situation, or thing that has been lost. Often, if the anger is directed toward what is really causing the griever to be angry, the anger subsides sooner and other emotions can surface as well.

When a griever feels heard and understood, the Angry dwarf can be at home without taking over the house. A supporter's receptive listening can go a long way toward making Angry a sporadic visitor rather than a permanent resident.

#7: *Gloomy*

Gloomy is the first dwarf to come and the last to leave. He's the guest you'd most expect, but often grievers aren't prepared for his comings and goings. Sometimes, things seem fine, and then, out of the blue, Gloomy appears in full force. Other times, when the griever expects to feel sad, Gloomy is nowhere to be seen. Gloomy is unpredictable.

Another thing about Gloomy is that he loves to get together with his buddies, Worry, Empty, Lonely, and Guilty, for unhappy hour. And watch out for the hangover—when sadness is combined with fear, guilt, loneliness, and emptiness, hopelessness can set in.

Supporters can help by recognizing the presence of sadness and providing a safe emotional space for grievers to feel and express sadness. It may be uncomfortable to sit in the presence of others' pain—especially when there is little we can do to make the pain go away. But to sit with others and let them know that they are not suffering alone is to give a true gift. As supporters, we need to give up the need to "fix" or to feel like we've said something wonderful or done something perfect. We need to acknowledge our own limitations in the face of overwhelming grief. Sometimes just being there is enough.

There are times, though, when the care that supporters can give is not enough. When there are ongoing, long-term signs of serious depression, such as prolonged despair, changes in sleep patterns and appetite, inability to concentrate, substance abuse, feelings of worthlessness or hopelessness, or talk of suicide, the griever may need professional help. In this case, a supporter may help by suggesting a clergy person, counselor, psychologist, or psychiatrist and, with the griever's agreement, taking steps to get professional support.

walking the grief pathway
With the Dwarfs

So now you have met the Seven Dwarfs of Despair. Accompanying a griever along the road of grief means allowing for and expecting these other companions along the way. Knowing and recognizing these grief companions can help supporters to invite others into the mix—Empathy, Solidarity, Sanity, Serenity, Tranquillity, Memory, and Possibility. With these companions nearby, the griever is better able to achieve the goal of grief.

The Goal of Grief

The goal of grief is to gradually detach enough from the loss
so as to form new and life-giving attachments with other persons
and things. Grieving is a process that will enable the one
who has suffered loss to get to a place of greater acceptance
and peace. Life will go on. And the truth is, so will the
grieving. Grieving never completely ends. There will always,
in some way, be lingering grief.

The goal of grief is not to completely let go of the person,
the situation, or the object that has been lost. What once
was, what has been lives on in memory. Reattaching to other people and things just means that *what was* is no longer
dominant. But *what was* does not go away. The goal of grief
is to embrace *what is* and *what will be*...without
having to completely part with what has been.

As Anne Lamott said in her "Homage to Age and Femininity"
in *O Magazine:* If you haven't already, you will lose someone you can't live without, and your heart will be badly
broken; and the bad news is that you never completely get
over the loss of a beloved person. But this is also the good
news. They live forever, in your broken heart that doesn't
seal back up. And you come through. It's like having a leg
that never heals perfectly—that still hurts when the weather
is cold—but you learn to dance with the limp.

chapter three

supporting the

Grieving

Being Present Through Times of Grief

Now that we've considered the basics of loss and grief and met the Seven Dwarfs of Despair, in this chapter, we'll look at general ways to support those who are grieving. Then, in Chapter 4, I'll offer specific ways to be supportive in list form. In Chapters 5-10, we'll focus on specific losses, feature accounts from people who have suffered these particular losses, and provide additional support suggestions appropriate for each situation.

Be-Attitudes

"Blessed are they who mourn, for they shall be comforted."
I first heard this verse when I was little, but it has stayed
with me. I've always understood these words as a kind of
promise in the universe that those who are profoundly sad
and deeply despairing will not suffer alone. This verse is
one of a list of "Beatitudes" found in the Bible. *Beatitudes* is
a term derived from the Latin *beati*, which means "blessed"
or "happy." Though the verse promises that those who
mourn will be comforted, it doesn't specify *how* one can
provide comfort. Knowing how to offer comfort to those
who mourn helps to facilitate their grieving processes
and move them toward healing and wholeness.

And so I offer a description of four *Be-Attitudes*—helpful
ways to be when reaching out to others in times of loss.
These Be-Attitudes suggest appropriate attitudes and actions
in an order that coincides with typical stages of grief.
Keep in mind, though, that every person's grief process
is individual and seldom linear. Use these attitudes gently,
knowing that the goal is for the griever to appropriately
separate from the loss and reattach to other people and
things in life-giving ways.

The To-Be List in the following chapter offers suggestions
for support corresponding to the attitudes.

be-attitude #1: *Be Appropriate*

The first Be-Attitude has to do with being appropriate to the level of relationship. Each of us has a range of relationships. We are closer to some family members than others. We have inner-circle and outer-circle friends. We have neighbors we wave to before driving in the garage and closing the door, and neighbors we can call on at midnight when we're locked out. Then there are the neighbors who at midnight, when you're locked out, put on a pot of decaf and break out the good chocolate. We have co-workers who get a smile and others who get the inside story every time.

Determining the amount of closeness in the relationship between supporter and griever can help the supporter determine the appropriateness of support to offer during a time of loss. If the relationship is casual, then offering to do helpful tasks is a good start. If the supporter and the griever know one another in the context of an organization— a workplace, club, or charity, for example—then offering to help with organizational tasks is a good place to start. If the supporter and griever have often spent time in one another's home, then offering to help with house-related chores may be appropriate.

If the relationship is close, then the supporter is in a position to create a safe space for the griever to share the ongoing effects of grief. The intimate-level supporter has the most opportunity to be attuned to the presence and effects of the

Seven Dwarfs of Despair—Spacey, Lonely, Empty, Guilty, Worry, Angry, and Gloomy (Chapter 2).

That's not to say that the supporter's role can't change. Often, loss and grief can cause change in relationships— people who were more distant become closer and assume a role of significance. Conversely, people who were once close become more distant. By paying attention to the signals and cues the griever is sending, the supporter can better determine ways to be responsive all along the journey of grief. If asked, the griever will usually let the supporter know ways to be helpful. Or the supporter can go ahead and do supportive actions as they seem appropriate. Feedback from the griever will inform other actions. A supporter's evolving role in the grief journey will continue to be defined as the supporter continues to pay attention to the griever's evolving needs.

Part of being appropriate is being realistic about what we as supporters can do. As stated in Loss Lesson #4, there are limitations to a supporter's role. Those limitations, discussed in Chapter 1, include the inability to take away the pain of the loss. No one can do that. Through the grief process, the pain is contextualized; it becomes part of the griever; it lessens in significance and intensity; it gets transformed to the healthy place of memory. All this happens in grief's sweet time, on the griever's individual timetable. The supporter provides crucial support along the way, but the supporter cannot actually take the pain away.

There are other limitations to a supporter's role. There's the limitation of knowledge and skill. Most supporters are not trained grief counselors, psychologists, or therapists. This is an okay thing! The supporter is not to provide counseling or therapy. It is important that supporters remember this distinction—supporters are not there to be therapists. Supporters are there just to *be there*—to accompany the griever in appropriate, genuine, responsive, respectful ways along the journey of grief.

In addition to the limitation of role, there is the very real limitation of time. It is not a supporter's duty to devote his or her whole life to supporting the grieving. The supporter has a life—and that life must continue to be lived as fully and joyfully as possible. A supporter need not do all that the griever needs done—but may be able to help to find other support for the griever. One of the best things a supporter may do is to help widen the circle of support—through personal relationships or through support agencies. We live in the real world, and time is a factor. Doing what is most needed in the time available can be very helpful to the griever.

Another limitation can be distance. Oftentimes, the ones providing support live across a large metro area or across the country. Physical acts of support and responsiveness are not an option. This is a very real factor in our mobile society. Still, people can support from afar, often in the form of cards, notes, delivered flowers, contracted services, phone calls, and e-mails. Presence along the grief journey need not be in person to be effective.

Along with the necessity of being realistic, there is another dimension to being appropriate—the need to be real. Supporters are most effective when they are genuine and authentic in their expressions of care. Sometimes people feel uncomfortable being in supportive roles, because they feel that they do not have the gifts or skills to adequately provide support. Someone may be great with tools but not so great at asking sensitive questions and listening empathetically. Such a person could better and more comfortably serve a grieving widow by offering to do minor household repairs than by sitting with her while she cries. A person who loves to bake can support a griever by dropping off a loaf of homemade bread. The point is that supporters can best support when they are acting in areas of their interests and abilities.

That is not to say that supporters cannot be stretched outside their comfort zones—they should be and they will be just by engaging in the grieving process. In the face of loss, no one is completely comfortable. Suggestions offered in this book should help supporters to feel more equipped to initiate support. When supporters act in ways that are genuine and true to who they are, both the supporter and the griever can feel more at ease. As long as supporters offer support that is appropriate to their skill levels and appropriate to the amount of time they can give without causing undue duress, ongoing support is a realistic and rewarding endeavor.

Another aspect of being appropriate has to do with giving or lending monetary or material assistance. Often supporters feel they could help those suffering the effects of loss by giving or lending money or things. A few cautions must be considered. First, supporters should remember that their role is not to take away the pain, but rather to accompany another along the journey of grief. Second, if supporters give financial or material assistance, they should realize that such means of support could put a strain on the relationship. If assistance is given in the form of a loan, there can be tension around when and how the loan is repaid. Often it is recommended that supporters give gifts instead of loans to avoid the stress around repayment. But supporters should realize that even gifts could cause relational stress. Giving gifts can cause the recipient to feel indebted and can sometimes cause supporters to feel resentful. Financial and material gifts can negatively affect previously mutual and reciprocal aspects of the relationship. If supporters do decide to lend or give financial or material assistance, they should do so knowing the risks involved.

> **Supporters should always have the grievers' needs at heart.**

The last word on being appropriate has to do with whose needs are being met. Supporters should always have the grievers' needs at heart.

"What is best for the griever?" should be the operative question. We all have the need to be helpful, the need to feel we are making a difference. But supporters need to make the need to be helpful secondary to the needs of the griever. We supporters need to make supportive gestures not to make ourselves feel good as much as to truly help the grieving. One young widow who lost her husband said she resented people who hurriedly called from their cell phones in between appointments to check in with her. "I could tell that they didn't really want to know how I was doing—they just wanted to feel like they were doing something good, and I resented it. If they really cared about how I was doing, they would have taken time to really listen to what I was going through." Supporters can help in appropriate ways by asking the griever what he or she needs, by listening attentively to the answers, and by being fully present—either physically, in phone calls, through notes and e-mails—and accompanying the person along the long road of grief.

#2: Be Responsive

The second Be-Attitude is to *Be Responsive*. This is an attitude that inspires action. This attitude suggests that supporters (responding to their areas of giftedness and limitation) should be present, proactive, and responsive to needs the griever may have. To be responsive, one must be attentive to the particulars of need as the grief journey progresses. But paying attention to the grieving is not a natural tendency. Often the natural tendency is to avoid the grieving.

When we hear of a loss, we often don't know what the right thing to do would be. Loss is always hard. Some losses—like death—are irrevocable. They change life forever. In the face of loss, we may not know how to respond. We're afraid we may say or do the wrong thing. So we may do nothing, or we may avoid the griever so we can avoid our own awkwardness.

A griever needs help and support all along the grief journey, though the nature of these needs will change. Immediately following the loss, there is often much to do to negotiate the life changes the loss may bring. Death brings the need for funeral arrangements as well as the ongoing tasks involved in learning to carry on without a significant other. Divorce brings the need to settle property, make custody arrangements, and accommodate new ways of living. Retirement often means doing financial planning to make up for lack of income. Property loss necessitates dealing with insurance agents and making efforts to replace what has been lost. The challenge of mounting tasks is greater, because this is the time that Spacey, the Dwarf of Despair, moves in and brings with him the haze of shock, confusion, denial, and numbness. Even simple tasks can seem overwhelming. Help with the extra tasks is often appreciated.

The need for help with loss-related and everyday tasks is amplified because grievers at this early stage need space and time. They need an excused absence from everyday duties and obligations. People who are grieving should be allowed the opportunity to do as little as possible so that they can feel the pain of their loss. This feeling of pain is productive—it aids the grieving process.

Grievers who feel they must stay busy distract themselves from the pain. Distraction slows the grieving process. The Empty, Lonely, and Gloomy dwarfs, if forced to the basement, will work together to plot their takeover at a later time when the griever least expects it.

What matters, then, is helping grievers to find time and space to process and deal with their loss. Being sensitive to grievers' individual and specific needs is key. One area of importance concerns communication. In times of loss—caused by illness, divorce, death, disaster, or other factors—ongoing communication is often necessary. Supporters want to know what is going on so that they can know how to be of assistance. It is helpful to ask how the griever would like to be in communication. Some people welcome phone calls, whereas for others, the phone is an intrusion and e-mail is preferred. Being appropriate and responsive in communication, as in other areas of support, has to do with asking grievers their preferences and being responsive to those requests.

From a Woman Whose Husband Suffered a Life-Threatening Illness

When my husband became seriously ill, family and friends were naturally concerned about him and interested in his progress. How to share information about his condition with all of them, as well as how to communicate their concerns and good wishes to him, soon became a difficulty on top of everything else. I could have spent hours a day just making and fielding phone calls.

Indeed, the cell phone was my lifeline for outgoing messages, and I often called friends and family members when I truly wanted or needed to talk—from a hospital lobby, a treatment waiting room, a parking lot, or wherever I happened to be. However, I didn't particularly like receiving phone calls, which always seemed to arrive at an inconvenient moment with an annoying jangle. My spouse didn't want to talk on the phone at all. So, as kindly as I could manage, I quickly and firmly discouraged everyone from making phone calls to me and, particularly, to the patient.

I'm more of an e-mail person, so I chose to use an e-mail list as a way of reaching out. One message, many recipients. Sometimes I would write one message and then tailor it for individual recipients. I could print out incoming e-mail messages for my spouse to read. Occasionally, people would send e-cards, which I would show him on the screen of my laptop.

Most of all, my husband and I appreciated cards and notes. These could be read and visually enjoyed all the time. A card or note with a phone number and an e-mail address in it reminded me to follow up with an outgoing call or to add someone's name to my e-mail address list.

As grievers progress along the journey of grief, their needs for support change. Whereas they needed supporters to do things for them in the early stages, they become more and more able to do things for themselves. After the do-for stage, grievers become ready for the do-with stage—when supporters invite grievers to join together for tasks, social events, and memory-sharing sessions (see the Be Inviting section). Supporters can sense when grievers are ready to do more for themselves by empathetically listening and being receptive to where grievers are in the grief process, which leads to the third Be-Attitude.

#3: Be Receptive

The third Be-Attitude is probably the most challenging, the one for which we are least equipped. *Being Receptive* is all about creating an open space for the griever to completely express his or her honest feelings. Creating the space for such an honest account of deep, tender feelings is largely dependent on the relationship that the supporter and griever had before the loss. The closer they were before, the more likely it is that kind of communication can happen. Still, even if the supporter and griever were close before, a new level of safety must be attained in this postloss time of life.

Creating a safe, open space for the griever is to have no goal other than being present and receptive for whatever the griever wants to say, feel, emote, or not say, feel, or emote. Creating a safe, open space has nothing to do with a specific space or place, but rather the caring and receptive demeanor of the supporter. Creating a safe, open space is showing a willingness to just be with the griever—to sit with the person in his or her pain.

Most of us have very little training, if any, on the art of being present in the face of another's pain. The truth is, someone else's pain and suffering makes us uncomfortable. We want to help. We want to make it better. We want to fix it! Loss presents situations that cannot be readily, easily, or quickly fixed. The hard truth is that many losses change life forever—often not for the better. To sit with another in his or her pain is to admit our raw vulnerability to the essential truth that such pain could inflict itself on our loved ones, on us. We want to avoid this ugly truth—or at least sugarcoat it enough to think that the pain can be lessened. Before we can sit with another in his or her pain, we must be willing to face the essential truth that loss and grief are a part of life. It's not for the faint of heart, but a willingness to be present and receptive to another in his or her pain is the greatest gift a griever can receive.

Creating a safe, open, emotional space involves listening. It means truly taking in all that the griever is experiencing. To listen with the goal of truly understanding what the other is feeling is to try to step out of one's own thoughts and experiences. This can be quite difficult, because often, in seeking to understand, we try to find common experiences to which we can relate. We try to understand by seeing the other's experience through the lens of our own experience. In order to be the most effective at listening, though, we need to realize the limits of engaging through our own perspectives.

There are experiences to which we cannot possibly relate, no matter how hard we try. In sensitive experiences of loss, it can be helpful to try to set our own experiences aside long enough to receive and understand the experience of the griever. We can seek to listen with *empathy*. The true meaning of empathy is not to relate to another's experience. When we relate based on our own experience, we are limited to how *we* would experience the loss. The griever experiences the loss differently. The true meaning of empathy, then, is *to search one's way into the experience and thoughts and feelings of another*. To enter another's experience is to leave our own experiences behind, at least for this time of receptive listening. This means that the response "I know how you feel" is not particularly helpful. A limitation in providing support is that we *don't* know how the griever feels. But with empathetic listening, we are more able to search our way into understanding.

Creating a safe, open, emotional space involves receiving
any displays of emotion. We're not used to seeing someone
in a complete rage. But, when given a safe space, often
a griever will be furious with the funeral director, with the
neighbor who didn't express condolences, with the deceased
for leaving her behind with the house renovation half done,
with herself for not having insisted that he go to the doctor.
When given a safe space, a griever may sob and convulse
with emotion. When given a safe space, the griever may
express sheer terror about the future. Or a griever may sit in
silence, not wanting to speak, but grateful for the company
of another. A careful, full-of-care listener will provide an open,
caring, receptive space for whatever is or is not expressed.

Supporters are not used to seeing raw displays of emotion.
Often we don't engage in close conversations with grievers
because we are afraid we will not know how to respond if,
in fact, the griever does break into convulsive sobs or a fit of
anger. In any display of extreme emotion, a supporter need
only nod and murmur supportive sounds: "Yes, I know."
"I'm here." "You're okay." "I know it hurts." The supporter
can be extremely helpful in extreme displays of emotion by
being the "calm in the emotional storm." If a supporter does
witness an extreme display of emotion, the supporter can
know that he or she has, indeed, provided a safe emotional
space for the griever to release deep emotions.

The griever needs to know that he or she will not be judged for displays—or lack of displays—of emotion. (Some grievers feel guilty that they don't or can't cry.) Remember, the griever is keeping close company with the Guilty dwarf. Guilty is questioning everything that the griever did or didn't do to cause or worsen the loss. Guilty is also harping on the way the griever is handling the grieving process, saying things like, "You should be handling this better." "You should be over this by now." "You're acting like a crazy person." The griever can feel ashamed of overwhelming, confusing, or guilty feelings. The more real the griever can be, the more he or she can feel acceptance for all he or she is feeling in this stage of grieving; the more these feelings can be expressed and heard, the more effective the grieving process will be.

Responses to expressions of anger, sadness, fear, and guilt can and should be minimal and genuine. A simple "Yes, yes" or "I hear you" or other murmurs of understanding are adequate. Responses are not what is needed. It is the supporter's engaged, receptive presence that is the most helpful.

Responses that are not helpful are attempts to offer inappropriate comfort. Often those trying to be supportive will offer trite phrases, such as "Time heals all wounds" or "He's in a better place" or, even worse, "It was God's will." Such responses are an attempt to put a bandage on the hemorrhaging wound. Trying to stop the emotional bleeding with inadequate stopgap measures only impedes the productive grieving process. Instead of letting the wound bleed and heal naturally, trite words and phrases suggest that the wound really isn't that bad. Also, trite responses such as "It was for the best" demonstrate a lack of engaged, receptive presence. They show no real attempt by the supporter to search the way into the experience of another. Often such phrases are used because supporters just don't know what to say. Remember that it is okay to say nothing or next to nothing. It is enough just to be there.

Misguided attempts to take away the pain are often attempts to make ourselves feel better, in that we have been effective in offering comfort. Additionally, attempts to make the person feel better are attempts to avoid having to witness this pain. Being truly receptive and open to another means letting go of our own need to immediately make someone feel better.

Creating a safe space involves allowing room for silence. Sometimes—maybe much of the time—the griever may not feel like talking. Processing grief is a lonely endeavor. It is very self-oriented and requires shutting out the world so as to heal the interior spaces and develop a new sense of self. This is solitary work, and it carries with it the danger of the griever isolating himself or herself. It can be a gift to allow someone to be silent but not alone. The silence need not be empty silence—it is filled with care and support.

Creating a safe space often involves letting the griever draw on the supporter's strength for a while until he or she is strong enough to emotionally support himself or herself. A supporter can often tell when a griever is emotionally self-supporting when the pain of the past loss no longer prevents normal functioning. The griever will seem more himself or herself. Normal activities will once again bring pleasure. There will often be more of a willingness to reengage in life. Dinner invitations may be accepted more often. An exercise routine may be resumed. Food starts to taste good to the griever again. Any signs of reentry into life can be taken as positive signs.

Getting to the place of detaching enough from the loss to reattach to other people, situations, and things takes energy, time, and, most definitely, support. In a safe space filled with the receptive support of another, the diminished self has the greatest chance to emerge.

#4: *Be Inviting*

The fourth Be-Attitude involves being inviting. Essentially, what the supporter is doing is helping to invite the person back into a life lived in the present, with hopes for the future as opposed to a life lived looking at the past.

Recall that the goal of grieving is that the griever will receive enough emotional release from the loss so as to reattach to other people, situations, and things. As stated earlier, the loss never goes away. It is, as Anne Lamott said, having a limp and still being able to dance.

One way that the effects of the loss can be lessened is for the loss to more and more be seen in past tense, as a part of life that once was. When the loss is moved into the "memory" category, one can more fully look ahead to the future with hope.

A significant way in which a supporter can be helpful to a griever is to invite memories. This can work whether or not the supporter knew the person or situation. If the supporter did know the deceased or shared experiences before the loss, both supporter and griever can reminisce. If not, the supporter can invite memories and stories. Each time the griever talks about the situation or person in the past tense, there becomes more and more of a delineation between what was and the present (what is), along with the future (what is yet to be).

Often people wanting to support the grieving will discourage the recounting of memories for fear that it will evoke the pain of the loss. The opposite is true, however. Though remembering can, indeed, be painful at times, it falls in the "productive pain" category.

The supporter can further invite conversation around memories by engaging in memory-related activities. The supporter could offer to help put together a memory book or encourage the griever to write in a journal. The supporter could ask about memorabilia in the griever's home. By talking about past experiences in the past tense, the griever is more able to weave together his or her past with the present. That integration is a major step toward healing and wholeness.

Inviting memories can be helpful all along the grief journey. Remembering important events and holidays is a significant way in which supporters can aid the grieving process. When the loss involves a death, every holiday is different. Especially during the first year after the death, a card on the holidays, acknowledging the way the holiday will be different without this special person, will be very appreciated. Similarly, a card sent to mark the deceased person's birthday would be a very thoughtful touch. For those who have recently gone through a divorce, the time around the wedding anniversary could be a time when the griever needs support. Cards that say "Thinking of you during this time" are gentle, caring gestures.

Another way the supporter can be inviting is by extending invitations for the griever to participate in activities, to reengage in life. The sensitive supporter will pay attention to what the griever may like to do, or may have done once upon a time, and suggest activities with these thoughts in mind. As time passes following the loss, the griever may be more willing to try something new or try something again that hasn't been done in a long time. My friend Joan, once a concert violinist who gave up playing when she had children, took up the violin two years after her divorce. The joy she feels while playing in the community orchestra is "indescribable," she says. "It's like a part of my past has come back to life." Her circle of friends, who watched a significant part of her die during the divorce, is pleased to see her engage in her former passion.

Being inviting means being sensitive to the person's particular situation and stage in the grief process. A newly divorced person might appreciate an invitation to a dinner out, but it may be awkward if the others are all married couples. A person going through chemo may be too exhausted to go out for dinner—lunches may be better. A person who is trying to reengage in life may appreciate an invitation to do something physical to get back in shape. The key to appropriate invitations is being attentive to the person's needs and creative about meeting those needs in ways that increasingly involve being out in the world.

When supporters are aware of these four ways of being present to those who are grieving—being appropriate, being responsive, being receptive, and being inviting—they can offer support from a more informed and, hopefully, more comfortable place. In the next chapter, you will find a list of specific suggestions based on each of the four Be-Attitudes.

chapter four *the*
To-Be List

Specific Ways to Be Helpful

In the first three chapters, we talked about principles of loss and grief and general ways to support those who are grieving. In this and the following chapters, I will suggest specific, concrete ways to be supportive to those who are grieving.

This chapter contains a To-Be List based on the Be-Attitudes presented in the last chapter. When people in your life experience loss, this general list can serve as a resource for ways you can reach out to them. Each situation of loss is different, as is each relationship between you and the victim of loss. Whenever loss occurs, scan this To-Be List and choose the suggestions that feel the most appropriate for the particular situation and relationship.

Be Aware of the Goal of Grief

When supporting those who are suffering effects of loss, it is helpful to be aware of the goal of good grief work. The goal of grief is for the griever to *eventually* detach enough from the loss so as to form healthy, life-giving attachments with other significant people, situations, and things.

Be Appropriate to Your Relationship

ways to be supportive to others in times of loss:

- Be respectful of and responsive to the griever's needs.

- Consider the nature of your relationship with the griever.

- Offer support consistent with your previous ways of relating.

  - If your relationship is more functional and pragmatic, offer functional and pragmatic support.

- If your relationship has been close, offer more intimate support.

- Offer support in ways that are appropriate to the griever's and your areas of commonality.

  - If you work together, offer to help in work matters.

  - If you are neighbors, offer to mow the lawn or do child care.

  - If you know each other from a health club, suggest a game of tennis.

  - If you volunteered in a theater league, invite the griever to see a play.

- Be aware of whose needs are being met. Put the griever's needs before your own need to be helpful.

  - If the griever says he wants to be alone, respect his wishes.

  - If the griever says he does not want food, don't deliver it anyway.

  - If the griever does not want to communicate by phone, send cards or e-mails even if the phone is your preferred way of communication.

- Be respectful of the griever and the progress being made along the grief journey.

  - At the beginning of grief, do tasks *for* the griever.

  - As the griever is able to do more for himself or herself, do tasks *with* the griever.

  - Invite the griever to share in activities as he or she is ready.

  - Invite the griever to share memories of who or what was lost.

- Be you. Be real.

  - Know your strengths.

  - Know your limitations.

  - Be realistic about what you can do, given your own commitments and demands.

  - Be careful not to give more than you can and still maintain your own physical and mental well-being.

  - Know that even in our limitations, our gentle, caring presence can offer immense comfort and facilitate effective grieving.

- Be aware of the goal:

  - That the griever reconnect with himself or herself in a way that leads to greater confidence and competence in life.

Be Responsive to the Griever's Needs
(the "doing for" stage)

- Respond promptly on first hearing of the loss.

- Ask how the person is doing.

- Express genuine sympathy and show genuine concern.

- Speak openly and directly about the loss.

- If you have experienced a similar loss, bring it up after you have listened to the other person's account. Only discuss your loss if it seems to be helpful to the griever.

- Cry if you feel like crying.

- Ask how you can be helpful.

- Offer to do tasks that you think might be helpful. Suggestions:

  - Mow the griever's lawn.

  - Shovel the driveway.

  - Weed the garden.

  - Watch the kids.

  - Take care of carpool duty.

  - Pick up groceries or run other errands.

  - Do work-related tasks for a co-worker.

  - Help to clean a room, closet, or garage.

  - Offer to pay for a cleaning service to clean the house, wash windows, organize a cluttered room.

- Just do it—suggestions for gestures to consider doing without asking:

  - Deliver a basket of warm muffins for breakfast.

  - Leave a basket of fresh vegetables from a local farmers' market.

  - Deliver a gift of age-appropriate toys or activities for the kids.

- Give or send a package of notes and stamps
  (the person may want to write thank-you notes).

- Drop off flowers from your garden, or send
  flowers or a plant—especially months after
  the loss when initial gestures have subsided.

- Be careful about giving financial or material assistance.

  - Gifts or loans can place strain on the relationship
    by creating a sense of dependency and/or resentment.

- Send cards and notes on an ongoing basis to let
  the griever know that he or she is in your thoughts.

  - Send cards or notes to commemorate special
    events and occasions that are meaningful to
    the griever (anniversary of death or loss, birthday
    of deceased, wedding anniversary, holidays, etc.).

  - Send written accounts of your memories
    of the person, situation, relationship,
    or object that was lost.

- If the griever is in high-functioning mode, working
  on overdrive to get everything done, offer assistance
  so that he or she has time and space to process the loss.

  - Give gifts of self-care, such as a massage, spa,
    or bath products.

- Give the gift of music.

- Be an advocate.

  - Offer to contact lawyers, financial consultants, police, insurance agents, adjusters, damage specialists.

  - Offer to help record and manage information.

  - Offer to give or lend needed provisions.

  - Encourage the griever to take care of himself or herself—proper nutrition, exercise, rest.

Be Receptive (the "being with" stage)

- Do not avoid the griever.

- Ask gentle, open-ended questions, for example:

  - How are you feeling?

  - What times of the day are the hardest?

  - How is sleeping for you?

  - What do you miss about him the most?

  - What do you fear the most?

- What did you like the most about the situation you are grieving?

- What makes you angriest right now?

- What part is the most overwhelming?

- What surprises you about how you're feeling?

- What does the pain feel like?

- Where does it hurt most?

- What do you miss the most?

- Are there any nagging regrets?

- How can I help?

- Make it obvious that you are there to listen.

  - Listen empathetically—search your way into the experience of the griever.

  - Allow for the sharing of any and all feelings and emotions, and receive them with gentle acceptance.

  - Respond with soothing words, "Yes," "I see," "There, there."

  - Allow for silence.

Know that the intensity
of grief fluctuates.

Know that the grief
journey is exhausting.

- Offer hugs.

- Arrange a time to meet again.

- Send cards as a way to offer your
  supportive presence without
  actually being present.

what NOT to do:

- Do not avoid the griever.

- Don't rush the conversations.

- Don't share your similar experience of grief or that
  of others until the griever has completely shared
  his or her experience. Only share if it seems to be
  received in a positive way.

- Don't say "I know how you feel."

- Don't offer false comfort to minimize the pain.

  - Don't say "She's in a better place," "Time
    heals all wounds," or "It was God's will."

- Don't minimize the loss.

  - Don't say "It's not that bad."

- Don't tell of people who've had it worse.

- Don't say "You'll be okay."

- Don't say "At least you have your health, other children, money in the bank," etc.

- Don't assume anything about the impact of the loss on the person. Only by listening can you really know the effects of the loss.

- Don't offer advice or quick solutions.

  - Don't say "I think you should..." or "If I were you..."

  - Don't try to hurry along the grieving process.

- Do not let the person become overly dependent on you to the point that it is not healthy for either of you.

Be sure to:

- Be observant for signs of serious depression:

  - Dramatic weight loss or gain.

  - Alcohol or drug abuse.

  - Pain or constriction in the chest.

- Disturbed sleep patterns.

- Ongoing signs of hopelessness or talk of suicide.

- Encourage griever to seek professional help if you suspect serious or ongoing depression.

Be Inviting (the "doing with" phase) invite memories:

- Invite memories through conversation (in person or otherwise).

  - If the loss involved a person, memory-related questions include:

    - How is life different for you now than it was before she died/you broke up?

    - What do you miss most?

    - How is the loss getting easier or harder?

    - When did you first meet?

    - What did you learn from one another?

- How did your relationship cause you to grow?

- How did you like to celebrate holidays?

- What were favorite things to do together?

● If the loss was situational, memory-related questions include:

- How are your days different now?

- What did you particularly like about the way things used to be? What did you dislike?

- How is this situation better or worse?

- What have you learned through the change?

- How have you grown?

- What about this new situation did you anticipate? What caught you by surprise?

● If the loss was a material object, memory-related questions include:

- What do you miss about the object?

- What did you especially like about the object?

- What made it unique?

- When did you first get it?

- How did it make you feel?

- How will you make sure you always remember it?

- For all kinds of losses:

  - Ask to see pictures or memorabilia of who or what is being remembered.

  - Give a memory book to preserve pictures and mementos of what was lost. Offer to help put it together.

  - Give a journal as a gift for the griever to record memories.

  - Give a beautiful frame for the griever to display a photo of what was lost.

  - Offer to make an audio recording of the griever talking about the person, situation, or object being remembered.

  - Send cards to share memories.

invite renewed participation in life:

- Ask the griever to accompany you to a movie, concert, lecture, church service, museum, garden tour, or restaurant, etc.

- Ask him or her to accompany you on a walk, run, hike, or bike ride.

- Suggest classes that you could attend together.

- Invite the griever to do common tasks together. Examples include:

  - Rake the griever's yard, then yours.

  - Have a closet-cleaning day—first hers, then yours.

  - Take both of your cars to a fancy car wash.

  - Invite the person and her kids to a new playground. Bring a picnic lunch.

  - Invite the griever to go shopping for anything from groceries to craft supplies to new clothes.

  - Invite the person to go on a day trip or a weekend away.

examples of ways to extend invitations:

- I have a friend who also lost her sister. Would you be up for coming over for a lunch with the three of us? I think she would really benefit from talking to you.

- I love to garden. What would you think about us planting a flower bed in honor of your beloved dog?

- Would you want to join me on a walk some morning or evening?

- There are some great local classes on hobbies we both love. Want to take a look at the catalog?

- I'd really like to stay connected, even though we live far apart. What would you think about scheduling times when we could regularly talk on the phone?

- I'd love to see pictures of your loved one. If you'd like to share, could we set up a time?

- Would you want to get together and make a memory book as a special way to remember life before the loss?

While being inviting, continue being open to hearing the emotional response to the challenges of engaging the present and facing the future while still bearing the hurt of the past.

Questions and Conversation Starters

Supporters long to comfort those who are grieving. "What can I do?" is a question often asked during times of loss. Supporters, especially those who are close to grievers, can often offer the most comfort by engaging in conversation with the griever. Some people avoid close conversation with those who are grieving because they don't know what to say, don't want to "open a wound," and because they are afraid of evoking an emotional response they feel ill-equipped to deal with. However, it is very helpful for those who are grieving to feel heard and understood in their experience.

Listed below are suggestions for conversation starters. Being in conversation shows that you care. The best response is careful, empathetic listening and comforting, nondescript phrases, such as "Yes, I know," "I'm so sorry," or "This is such a hard time." If the griever has a highly emotional response, the supporter can help a great deal by being the calm presence in the storm. Just being there—being there appropriately, showing respect, care, and sensitivity, is a wonderful gift that the supporter can give the griever.

conversation starters:

- I've thought of you ever since hearing of your loss. I hope you're doing okay.

- How are you feeling?

- How are you feeling, really?

- What would make today better?

- After this amount of time has passed, are there aspects of grief that are getting easier? Are there things that are more difficult?

- Are there times of the day/week/year that are harder or easier than others?

- I'm free all day Sunday. Is there something you'd like to get done that we could do together?

- How are your kids doing?

- Is there something I could do that would be helpful for the kids?

- What is particularly challenging right now?

- What has changed in your life?

- What do you remember most about the person/situation/thing you lost?

- What did you do with that person that made you laugh?

- I've heard that grief is like a roller coaster. Is it like that for you?

- I'd like to check in and just see how you're doing. Do you prefer phone calls or e-mail?

- What about your relationship with this person impacted your life the most?

- What about this person would you most like others to know?

- Did you get angry with each other? If so, what about?

- How did you grow from disagreements?

- How did you meet?

- What was your first memory of your significant other, situation, or object?

- What do you most enjoy about where you live now?

- Is there anything about being transferred that you look forward to?

- Of the things that were stolen, what do you miss most?

- What are your feelings about finding a new job?

- Tell me about what your house was like before the fire.

- What do you miss most about life before the wheelchair?

- If you still had your driver's license and could drive anywhere, where would you go? What is it like needing to get rides?

- Hope you know that I'm comfortable with **quiet**. I'm happy just to sit with you, if that's okay with you.

chapter five

Death

Supporting Those Who Grieve Various Death Situations

All losses can be significant and life-altering, but the finality of death can make this loss the most devastating. Many factors affect the grief journey following a death: The manner of death, the degree to which it was anticipated or not, and how close the survivor was to the deceased are but a few of the factors affecting grief. A key factor affecting the journey of grief is the kind of relationship that existed between the griever and the deceased. The more supporters of the grieving understand how various relationships affect grief, the more equipped they can be to offer support. Following are discussions of different types of relational loss due to death.

Pregnancy Loss

Pregnancy loss can be devastating. Anytime a pregnancy does not result in the birth of a healthy baby, deep and profound loss is experienced. The loss may be private if only the mother and father knew about the pregnancy or shared if siblings, grandparents, and other family members were joyously anticipating this new arrival. Miscarriage brings with it the loss of hopes, expectations, and dreams. Even if the mother is able to become pregnant again, one or both parents carry the fear that this pregnancy could also end in sadness. For many who experience loss during pregnancy, life is forever tinged with this sadness.

from a mother who miscarried:

I felt I was in some strange alternative universe where I had a huge, horrible, sad secret that no one else could know. After all, there had been no child to mourn, no one to name or bury or remember—except I remembered. I knew that child in my heart and was already in love.

from another mother who miscarried:

What you never hear about miscarriage, before you actually
have one, is just how agonizingly long it takes. I began
spotting at eight weeks gestation, but the major hemorrhaging wouldn't begin for another week, and it took three more
days after that before I actually lost the baby. All the while,
part of me was already resigning myself to the worst, while
the other part was hanging on like crazy to hope. When
I finally lost the baby, I just cried and hugged my husband
and said, "This is the worst thing that's ever happened
to me." At the time it definitely felt that way.

For the first few weeks after the miscarriage, I had to muster
up every ounce of will in order to "act natural" at work, which
was emotionally exhausting. I kind of wanted to tell the
people around me, but I wasn't willing to risk breaking down
into tears at work, so I kept it to myself. Also, the ordeal still
wasn't over. The bleeding continued, much like it does after
childbirth, only without the joy of a new baby to go with it.

It was all so draining—and disappointing. I hadn't realized
before I miscarried how many dreams I'd already built up
around this baby I had begun loving the moment I knew
I was pregnant. Also complicating things was the fact that
my husband got over the loss much more quickly than I did.
I was still grieving months later. He had moved on. When
I did get pregnant again, I was a nervous wreck throughout

the first trimester and wouldn't allow myself to get my hopes up—before I started dreaming about this baby.

from the journal of a man whose wife miscarried:

9-19-88. I am thinking about you today, Mary Regina, on this third anniversary of the night we lost you forever. You would have been two years seven months old by now. Toilet-trained and talking. Full of fun and mischief. An angel when asleep. An angel when awake. In my mind, I can see me doing for you the things a daddy should do. Holding you on my lap in my big corduroy chair, strapping you into your car seat, hoisting you into the shopping cart at Farmer Jack's while saying, "Such a big girl!" I always think of you as having reddish blond hair like your sister's. Blue eyes, of course. There, at the end of the hall by the clothes hamper, you sit on the floor, wailing about the toy Kelly grabbed from you. I come, full of sympathy, lift you and hold you near, feel the cool skin of your cheek against mine and the wet trace of your tears. God bless you, my daughter…"

The To-Be List in Chapter 4 contains actions and attitudes that are generally appropriate for many types of loss. Those included here are specifically helpful for the loss of a pregnancy.

support for loss of pregnancy:

- Ask the mother how she and the father are doing.

- Don't neglect the dad, especially if you are close to him, in expressions of care.

- Don't assume that miscarriage is easier to cope with than a stillbirth or neonatal death. At whatever point the loss occurs, the result is the loss of the baby.

- Don't assume that there will be another pregnancy.

- Don't try to cheer the parents up.

  - Don't say anything that resembles "This was for the best."

- Don't minimize the loss.

  - Don't say "At least you didn't know the baby."

  - Don't say that the parents are lucky to have other children.

  - Don't say "You're young enough to have other children."

- Don't feel guilty if you're expecting a child or if you have children.

- Don't forget that the grievers' children have lost a sibling. Ask the parents how you can best support the children.

supportive responses:

- "I'm so sorry about your miscarriage."

- "I know how much you (and your husband) wanted this baby."

- "How are you feeling now?"

- "Can I call you next week to see how you're doing?"

- "I really don't know what to say about such a great loss."

- "Know I'm keeping you and your family in my prayers/heart."

supportive gestures:

- Send cards or notes:

  - In the months after the loss to offer care and support.

  - Around the time of the due date.

- On other occasions:

  - Mother's Day for the mom.

  - Father's Day for the dad.

  - The anniversary of the due date.

- Suggest framing a sonogram picture.

- Suggest planting a rosebush or a tree to memorialize the baby.

Loss of a Child

No parent should have to experience the death of a child. It seems to go against the natural order of things. Children are supposed to outlive their parents. They are supposed to live happy, healthy lives that go on long after the parents are deceased. But it doesn't always happen that way. As discussed in Loss Lesson #1, Loss Happens. Even devastating loss. Even loss that is beyond what one could imagine.

When a parent loses a child, the disbelief and shock can be overwhelming. The shock can be worse if the loss is sudden and/or violent. The loss is compounded by the death of parents' and other family members' hopes, expectations, and dreams for the child (however old the child may have been at death). The anger at the apparent injustice of it all can be debilitating.

The effect of a child's death is further complicated by the parental role: Parents often assume that it is their duty to protect their child—no matter how grown-up the child may be. Parents may feel a sort of responsibility for the child's death, no matter how irrational that may seem. Guilt can be a constant companion for the grieving parent. A parent can feel like he or she has lost a significant part of his or her identity with the loss of a child.

from a mother whose daughter died:

One of the best things that others did for me was to continue to socialize with me. Friends invited me out to lunch, neighbors made sure my husband and I were included in the neighborhood get-togethers, etc. What was most important was that I was not shunned because I was grieving. My friends were willing to grieve with me by inviting my presence.

One of the most thoughtful ideas was from a family that offered to host a birthday party on our daughter's first birthday following her death. They let us invite whomever we wanted, and the menu consisted of her favorite foods. They knew we would be thinking about her and the party we would have been having. So why not have a birthday commemoration party? Many of the guests brought gifts for me that were symbolic of my daughter.

Many people left notes and gifts at my daughter's gravesite. I felt very comforted by these gestures, because it was a sign that my daughter continued to be significant in the lives of others.

I found great comfort in the words "Life has not ended but merely changed" that were included in our religious rites. Thus I found hope and peace in the stories others would share with me of spiritual "encounters" they had with my daughter. These encounters as well as my own gave me a reason to believe these words of hope that my daughter's life went on, albeit in a different realm.

What wasn't helpful were comments such as "At least you have other children." "It was God's will." "God answers all of our prayers." "God only gives us what we can handle." When I heard these comments, I still missed dearly my daughter who died, and my other children could not take her place. As far as "God's will"—suffice it to say I found no comfort in those words. In fact, they seemed somewhat cruel. I did not pray for my daughter to die so, no, my prayers were not answered. As far as my coping abilities—I would prefer that God did not have so much faith in me.

In some instances, my husband actually saw people turn the other way and head in a different direction in order to avoid coming in contact with him. Not only did we lose a daughter, but we became social outcasts due to other people's fears.

It was not helpful when others tried to take away the pain or ignore the grief. There is a difference between comforting others in their grief and trying to remove the grief. Grief cannot be removed, but grievers can be comforted.

When I support others through grief, I know to validate the feelings and swings of emotion rather than trying to "make them better." I know to call the deceased person by name and share remembrances with his or her loved ones. I know that someone going through grief is constantly thinking about his or her loved one. I won't "remind" them by acknowledging their loss. I know that in the case of the loss of a young child, there is no rational, human explanation for why the child was not given the opportunity to grow into adulthood. Trying to find a reason is pointless.

The To-Be List in Chapter 4 contains actions and attitudes that are generally appropriate for many types of loss. Those included here are specifically helpful for the loss of a child.

support for loss of child:

- Do not avoid the grieving parents. Be present to their pain—as painful as it is to receive.

- Ask how both parents are doing.

- Realize that the death of a child often puts significant strain on the parents' relationship, as both parents grieve in different ways.

  - Listen with care.

  - It's okay to respond with tender silence.

  - Do not take sides.

  - Say, "This must be very hard for both of you."

- Talk about the child by name.

- Do not say, "I know/understand what you are going through" unless you have lost a child.

- Do not minimize the loss.

  - Do not say "He/she was spared the difficulties of adolescence/young adulthood/old age."

- Offer to do anything that will give the parents time and space to grieve.

  - If there are young children, offer child care.

  - Bring meals, do lawn or household chores, grocery shop, etc.

- Offer to find information about support groups of those who have experienced the death of a child.

- Offer to help preserve memories.

  - If you and the griever are close, offer to make a memory book together.

  - Give a journal to write thoughts.

  - Suggest planting a tree or rosebush to memorialize the child.

- Send cards:

  - In the months after the loss to offer care and support.

  - On the child's birthday.

  - At every holiday that was important to the family— Hanukkah/Christmas, Thanksgiving.

  - On other occasions, as appropriate, especially:

    - Mother's Day & Father's Day.

    - Around the anniversary of the child's death.

Loss of a Loved One
(parent, sibling, friend)

When people lose someone close to them, it is as if a part of them has died, too. Part of a person's identity comes from his or her relationships. When a person loses a loved one to death, a void is formed, an empty space once occupied by the important relationship. A griever never truly "gets over" the loss of someone significant but will learn to live with the loss. The goal of grief is for the griever to eventually detach enough from the loss to form attachments with other people in meaningful and life-giving ways.

from a young woman whose brother died:

My brother died in a drowning accident when I was 16 years old. He was 21. It's difficult to remember my mindset before his passing, because losing someone so close to you changes everything—the way you think and dream and interact and live. But I can recall that I never, ever imagined that I would experience the death of anyone in my immediate family—at least not when I was still young and growing, still trying to find my identity and place in the world. When he died, I thought this type of tragedy only happened to other people. And now my family was "the other people." After the funeral and initial weeks of our loss, correspondence from family and friends waned. People sort of forgot and moved on with their respective lives. It was difficult because, even though the funeral was over, the pain was still present and there was an apparent lack of a support system. My parents were extremely hurt by the diminishing concern, because their grief was so unbearable.

A lot of people don't know what to say, so they don't say anything at all. They act as if nothing happened and sweep it under the floor. Others, ignoring my brother and pretending he never existed, hurt me the most by far. I wanted to talk about him. I wanted to tell people about his personality and hobbies and about who he was. But I felt stifled and as if I would make the other person uncomfortable, so I kept my thoughts inside.

I have discovered throughout the years that there are three standard responses you receive when you disclose that you've lost a loved one. Some people will say they are sorry, others will ask what happened, and others will not respond at all. The third response is always the roughest. Initially, it was very hard when people were so uncomfortable that they didn't even try to be sympathetic, but instead dismissed my most life-changing event by ignoring or avoiding it.

After several years, I have reached a stage in my life in which I am content and just happy to have had time to heal and grow and work through my grief. I think about my brother every day. I miss him a lot. But I have hope that I will see him again one day in heaven, and that sustains me.

Loss of a Parent

When a parent dies, especially if this is the loss of the last surviving parent, the son's or daughter's position in life changes. Often, one who loses one or both parents describes feeling like an orphan, no matter his or her age or status.

Sometimes people feel that they shouldn't be so upset when a parent—especially an elderly parent—dies. After all, they reason, death is inevitable, and when one has lived a full life or when one has been sick, death can be expected. The idea that one should not be upset by death—even a seemingly inevitable one—is a myth. Attempts to dismiss the effects of the loss do not facilitate a healthy grief journey.

The reality is that the death of someone who has played such a significant part in one's life is profound. The parent who helped to shape the person's life will never again be physically present. This loss must be grieved. Supporters help to facilitate the grief journey by being present to all the emotions that surface through the deep loss of a significant loved one.

from a woman who lost her mother:

Three years after my mother's death, I still pick up the phone to call her without even thinking about it. I need a recipe, I want to tell her about the crocuses that are coming up early this year, I want to share something great that happened to my son—her grandson….I have my finger on the numbers. And then I remember. We talked every day when she was alive. I'd give anything to hear her voice one more time.

from a woman who lost both of her parents within four years:

What was not helpful to me was when others wanted to relive their grief experiences through mine. I didn't want to share theirs at the moment. I didn't want theirs to distract me from my own. It is not charitable to drone on and on about how your own parent passed. If you confronted someone lying in the road with multiple fractures, would you start telling them about your own? In the middle of childbirth, would you have wanted to have a friend in your room to share the details of her own? In pain—silence is your best friend. Helpful loving friends will be demonstrative in their caring rather than their words.

What was helpful? Cards with heartfelt thoughts and prayers…comforting hugs…friends showing up just to vacuum and dust while I sat in a near coma from my grief… those are who I remember most as being helpful. Soft, quiet guardians of my grief—they allowed me to cry, to remember, to share with them my parents, whom many had never met. I know now that I will never be anybody's little girl again. I will never hear my name—my full name, Sharon Ruth—in that special tone. The people who helped most quietly listened to my pain. They hugged softly and only when invited into my personal space. I hurt too much to be grabbed at and maneuvered into anything. Some came with photos of my parents—that was lovely. Some mailed them. I know that silence is a gift. I know that providing food—in the form of fruit, cookies, soft, easy-to-eat food—is a talent. Showing up and being invisible is a gift...a casserole left on the table with a note—and then disappearing...because it [support] is about the person being allowed and given permission to just sit and cry—and remember what he or she will never experience again...the sound, smell, touch, and feel of their loved one. Be kind—make their grief experience all theirs. Hopefully, someone will be kind enough to allow you the same when it is your time.

from a woman who lost her best friend:

Cards with handwritten memories of my friend helped and comforted and warmed my heart. I still have them all. I kept them out where I could see them. I take them out and read them from time to time. I feel the love toward my friend and toward me in those messages. Each is unique and personal.

from a man whose girlfriend died:

Time spent alone helped. Long walks. Macaroni and cheese. Hot showers. New music. Telling stories of my girlfriend and my adventures and laughing like crazy about how crazy we once were—all helped somehow.

The To-Be List in Chapter 4 contains actions and attitudes that are generally appropriate for many types of loss. Those included here are specifically helpful for the loss of a loved one.

support for loss of loved one:

- Talk directly and openly about the person who died.

- Remember that evenings, weekends, anniversaries, and holidays can be extra-challenging times.

- Check in through e-mail if you and the griever use it.

- Ask if the griever would like you to check in by phone. If so, call regularly (i.e., weekly) to check in.

- Help with domestic chores—offer to wash a car, mow the lawn, clean a kitchen, arrange for domestic help (pay for a one-time cleaning service), prepare and deliver meals or arrange for meal delivery service, etc.

- Encourage the griever to take care of himself
  or herself by giving massage/spa gift certificates
  or inviting him or her to do physical activity,
  such as going for a walk.

- Help the griever preserve memories of the departed.

  - Ask the griever to share stories about the deceased.
    Listen attentively—even to repeated stories.

  - Offer to help plant a tree or a rosebush
    in honor of the deceased.

  - Offer to help transfer photos to a DVD or movie.

- Send notes or cards to say you are thinking of
  the survivor, especially on poignant occasions—the
  deceased's birthday and important family holidays.
  Include memories you have of the deceased.

do not:

- Pry into personal matters.

- Offer advice.

- Minimize the loss by saying:

  - "I know how you feel."

- "At least he/she is not suffering."

- "Time heals all wounds."

- "He's/she's in a better place now."

- "It was God's will/timing."

- "Things will go back to normal before you know it."

Loss of a Spouse

A spouse's death can be one of the most profound losses ever experienced. In addition to the emotional loss to the surviving spouse, there are significant adjustments that must be made to many facets of daily life. All around are reminders of the spouse's absence. There's the chair where he used to sit, the flowers she used to water, the garage he kept so meticulous, the power tools she was so proud to master, the dog he used to walk, the things she used to take care of that he had no idea she did, the empty side of the bed.

Not only does the death of a spouse necessitate changes in countless aspects of everyday life, but it also often requires social, financial, and situational changes. Will the surviving spouse need additional income? Will the house be too much

for one to take care of? With the death of the "social plan-
ner," will the more introverted one who was left behind be
completely isolated?

For elderly persons who lose spouses, the loss can be even
more profound. Often, they have shared a lifetime, and one
may not remember how to function without the other. The
death of friends and siblings in their age group may mean
a smaller support group. Health challenges may compound
the difficulties of grieving.

For all these reasons, the death of a spouse is first on the list
of causes of major stress.

from a widow:

I wasn't prepared for the loss of friends. People who had
been "our" friends expressed sympathy in the weeks after,
but few contacted me again. At times, when I'd see some
of them at the gas station or out shopping, they would
speak but have trouble looking into my eyes. They seemed
relieved when they could take off. I've been given many
explanations for their behavior from grief counselors and
others, but it still hurts to think about it.

The people who didn't ask what they could do and went
ahead and did something—flowers, dinners, cards, help

with errands—those are the people I often remember with great affection. It's hard to ask for help. Many of us just can't—even when people say they're willing. I found it very easy and wonderfully comforting to simply accept a kindness offered.

The To-Be List in Chapter 4 contains actions and attitudes that are generally appropriate for many types of loss. Those included here are specifically helpful for the loss of a spouse.

support for loss of spouse:

- Ask how you can be helpful.

  - Immediately after the death, offer the surviving spouse assistance in tasks so that he or she can have needed time and space to grieve.

  - Realize that the deceased spouse may have taken responsibility for particular household tasks. In the early stages of grief, it is appropriate to "do for" the surviving spouse. Next, you could "do with"— teaching the griever how to do the activity, so that eventually the person is comfortable doing it on his/her own.

Examples:

- Grocery shopping

- Paying bills

- Organizing meals

- Housecleaning

- Yard work

- Making appointments with professionals (doctors, dentists, accountants, etc.)

- Home maintenance

- Auto maintenance

- Computer/technical support

- Driving/getting directions

- Making social arrangements

- Realize that the surviving spouse may need assistance with official and financial matters. These matters are private and personal. The surviving spouse may want the supporter's help, nonetheless. Or the supporter may assist (even from a distance) by helping to find lawyers, accountants, insurance agents, and others to offer assistance in the following:

- Notifying the Social Security office, business associates, organizations, banks, department of motor vehicles, credit cards, those holding bond and stock titles, real estate titles, etc.

- Changing bank accounts, attending to insurance matters, checking on mortgages and other loans, etc.

- Respect the surviving spouse.

  - Do not treat him or her as a child or as incapable.

  - Only do "for" the person so that he or she can have time to process grief. The goal is not to create dependency or to minimize competence.

  - Continually try to do what is needed— not what is too much.

- Talk often about the deceased spouse.

- Encourage the surviving spouse to share memories.

- Do not push the surviving spouse to clean out or give away the deceased's clothing and belongings. Leave it to the griever to decide the right time for that.

- Send cards.

  - Send thinking-of-you cards or notes immediately after hearing the news and for a year or so following the death.

  - Remember the birthday of the deceased and the couple's wedding anniversary.

  - Include specific memories of the deceased in cards and notes.

  - Send cards at holidays to acknowledge the difficulty the loss presents.

Loss of a Pet

Many people when hearing about the death of a pet consider the loss to be less significant or less life-altering than other losses. They may think that someone who has "just lost a pet" is not grieving and not in need of support. While this is sometimes the case, it is just as often, perhaps more often, incorrect.

Pets are frequently beloved companions, important members of the family. Pet owners celebrate their pets' birthdays, enjoy their company, display photos at work, carry photos in wallets, and tell others about their pets' antics, accomplishments, and intelligence. Pets provide companionship, emotional support, and unconditional love and acceptance. So it is no wonder that many people deeply grieve the loss of their pet. For a senior, coping with the loss of a pet can be particularly difficult, especially if the senior is living alone. For everyone who has deeply loved a pet, the loss is significant.

from a man who has lost two dogs to death:

One of the hard things about losing a pet, dogs in my case, is that many people don't understand the strength of the bond or the depth of the loss. If the loss were a human family member, everyone would understand. But people who don't have pets don't understand. Consequently, I have not felt like I can be open or communicative about the losses. Because of this, when others lose a pet, I reach out to them in a way that lets them know that I understand the significance of the loss. After losing the first dog, one understands that adopting another is like adopting a child you know will die in adolescence.

The To-Be List in Chapter 4 contains actions and attitudes that are generally appropriate for many types of loss. Those included here are specifically helpful for the loss of a pet.

support for loss of pet:

- If you don't have a pet and don't understand the pet-owner relationship, ask questions about the effects of the loss.

- Talk about the person's or the family's relationship with the pet.

- Suggest making a memorial for the pet.

- Give a frame as a gift to display the pet's picture.

- Give a memory book to preserve photos and other reminders—maybe the pet's collar, a piece of fabric from the pet bed, or a label from the pet's favorite food.

- If you knew and liked the pet, write a note about qualities you appreciated in the pet or memories you have.

- Send thinking-of-you cards or notes occasionally for a short time following the death to let the person or family know you remember their loss.

When a loved one dies, that person or animal can never be replaced in the hearts and lives of those in need of support. The loss is permanent. The good news is that when healthy grieving is allowed to happen, the griever can detach from the loss enough to significantly reattach to other people, situations, and things. One learns to live with the loss. In time—however long it takes—the pain of the loss ceases to dominate the present. The Dwarfs of Despair—Spacey, Angry, Empty, Lonely, Worry, Guilty, and Gloomy—still visit from time to time, but they are no longer dominant, controlling residents. The memory of the loss becomes a constant, often comforting companion along with the new dwarfs—Empathy, Solidarity, Sanity, Memory, Serenity, Tranquillity, and Possibility.

In the following chapters, we will consider suggestions for ways to be supportive in situations of loss other than death.

chapter six

loss of

Relationship

Divorce, Separation, and Breakup

We are relational people. We define ourselves
in and through our relationships. We are
a husband, a wife, a significant other to the
one to whom we are committed. We integrate
our partners into the patterns of daily life.
The things we do together, the ways in which
we communicate, the dreams and goals we
work toward all make us who we are as couples,
as members of groups, and as individuals.
The very way we regard our self-identities is
based on our relationships with others. When
a relationship ends, there can be a feeling of
loss of self. The way we see ourselves, the

way we spend our days, the way we relate to the world often must be redefined. The end of a relationship is often the end of a way of life. It is a death of sorts, a death of hopes and dreams.

The end of a relationship—divorce, separation, or breakup—involves aspects of choice. Choice is a complicating factor in relationship loss: one or both persons *choose* to end the relationship. Given that choice is involved, the grief responses at the end of a relationship may differ from the grief responses that occur as a result of death. If the decision to end the relationship is mutual, there may be less emotional turmoil. But if one person was the initiator, the grief response may be different for that person than it is for the other. Recall Loss Lesson #3—to look at loss from both sides and remember that the initiator and the one being left will deal with different aspects of loss, and their reactions may differ.

The person being left may take up immediate residence with the Angry dwarf. If given free rein, Angry may take over the household, causing the griever to focus all time and energy on rage at the initiator. Meanwhile, the initiator may be assaulted by Guilty. Guilty is persistent and may make frequent, unexpected showings, especially around matters relating to the children, if any. Empty and Lonely may move in quickly and stay long, or they may be pushed aside completely as one or both of the newly single people quickly jump into new relationships.

Worry is usually in constant contact, especially with the person who was left. Worry incessantly reminds about the changes that must now be addressed. In divorce or separation, there are changes to living situations, daily routines, finances, socializing, and future expectations. Breakups include all or some of these changes as well. Whether they have divorced, separated, or broken up, the parties may worry about again entering the dating world. Yes, the Worry dwarf has much on his mind.

Usually, Gloomy shows up—either immediately or eventually. It's not uncommon for either or both parties to feel much more despair a year after the breakup or divorce than what was felt immediately. The death of a relationship has complicated and ongoing emotional effects. Therefore, a productive grieving process is extremely important for healing to take place.

The death of a relationship, unlike the death of a person, does not come with traditional rituals to help navigate the loss. There is no established visitation time for others to surround the grievers with support and care. There is no funeral to mark a distinct end to a way of relating. There is no established pattern of sending cards and casseroles in the wake of the loss.

Supporters can be most helpful if they first abandon the idea that there is one right person and one wrong person involved in the end of a relationship. The less supporters choose sides, the more they can be helpful to both people. A good starting place for supporters is to refer to the *Be Appropriate* list in Chapter 4. Supporters can reflect on how close they were to the two ending the relationship. If supporters associated with both, it is appropriate to offer supportive gestures to both. Supporters can also try to respond to the needs of both parties by scanning the *Be Responsive* list in Chapter 4.

If a supporter is closer to one person than the other, it is appropriate to do more from the *Be Receptive* list for that griever. It is good to be receptive to whatever emotions are demonstrated in the grief process. Supporters are most helpful when they can listen without taking sides. Responding with phrases that acknowledge the emotion is all that is needed: "You sound very hurt and angry." "This is such a difficult time." "I hear you."

Divorce and breakups have two purposes: first, to dissolve a bond that has become less than fulfilling for at least one person and, second, to begin a new life. When both parties can effectively process the grief of their losses with the help of caring supporters, both can more easily begin a new life.

from a divorced man:

She was much more outgoing than I, the noisy life and soul of any gathering, a people magnet. I'm much more standoffish, quiet, solid. When news of our divorce became public, our friends and acquaintances from various social circles flocked to her, offering her all sorts of support and consolation. Immediately, I was the bad guy, isolated, not worth knowing, without support. I don't think she bad-mouthed me—well, not too much. But our so-called friends chose her automatically, regardless of any information. I was so damn angry. What right did they have to judge me in that way? And on what basis? No one asked me about years of marginalization, of her severe dose of princess-itis, of living as though she was owed everything, of her unwillingness to contribute equally financially or domestically to our life together.

from a divorced woman:

The choice to get a divorce was a difficult one, because I had two small children and really no visible means of support at that time. I felt as if I was losing a piece of me that had been such a part of my heart for so long, I didn't quite know how I would function at first. It was my choice to pursue the divorce. The most difficult part for me was giving in to the pain of having stayed for so long, uprooting my children from the home they had known and starting all over again. I didn't know what would happen to us. I just knew that being married felt like I had changed who I was to accommodate the husband I had chosen. Leaving was a retaking of myself. The problem was that I no longer knew who I was anymore! But I knew I had to find out.

What helped was joining a women's group to talk about all these issues I was facing. I formed a bond with another woman in the group, and we became sounding boards for one another. What didn't help was hearing how many people didn't like my husband when I was married to him. They couldn't wait to bash him once we were divorced. It didn't feel supportive; rather, it made me feel a bit like a fool that they knew (their words) it would never work out between us. They were just waiting for us to get divorced. I didn't get married with the thought of divorce as an out. I got married to stay married, so it felt more like an indictment of me than a support of me.

from a woman after a breakup with her boyfriend:

I was devastated. Just because it wasn't a marriage doesn't mean it isn't a loss, often a very significant one. Leaning on my girlfriends has gotten me through those times of hopelessness and broken dreams—sounds a little dramatic, but those are the emotions—girlfriends who have been on the same rocky road and have come out happy on the other side. These are the ones who know what to say. And when to take you out for drinks. These are the ones I call. What doesn't help: friends who have never been single as adults (meeting their future husbands in college and never otherwise being in the dating world) giving you advice about "love yourself first" or other BS. What the hell do they know? They are NOT the ones I call during these times.

from a woman whose partner left:

For weeks after my partner and I broke up, a pair of married couple friends took me under their wing. They invited me over to just hang out and play Scrabble and go for a ride and get ice cream. I knew I could call them and ask to come over for a while and they would be honored to have me. Priceless and so touching. I felt safe and held.

The To-Be List in Chapter 4 contains actions and attitudes that are generally appropriate for many types of loss. In addition, many of the supportive things suggested for those grieving the death of a spouse in the previous chapter are applicable, and those included here are specifically helpful for the loss of a relationship.

support for divorce/separation/breakup:

- If you were close to both parties, reach out to both through your presence, phone calls, e-mails, cards, and notes.

  - If you want to maintain relationships with both parties, don't take sides.

  - Let each know you are thinking of him or her.

  - Words that are spoken against the ex can be heard without being agreed with.

  - Respond with nods, silence, or with validations of the emotion:

    - "You sound very angry."

    - "That must hurt."

    - "This is such a difficult time."

  - Continue to initiate contact.

    - If you were closer to one than the other, your level of communication will probably be closer with that person, but the other need not be neglected.

- It's okay to let each know that you are
  reaching out to the other (and that you are
  not taking sides).

- Do not promote the idea that the griever start
  dating—let the griever decide when the time is right.

  - Realize that a new partner can be a sign that
    the former relationship is being put in the past
    and life is moving forward.

- Send cards or notes during the first year, especially
  at times that may be particularly sensitive, like
  the wedding anniversary and family holidays.

chapter seven

loss of

Employment

Supporting Victims of Job Losses

Work is a major part of life. What we do is a significant factor in who we are. In our society, we don't think twice about letting our job define us. I'm an accountant. I'm a nurse. I teach. I'm a server at a restaurant. I'm a welder. I'm a flight attendant. I'm a CEO. Our jobs become who we are and what we do. When our jobs are taken away from us, we may feel as if our very selves have been ripped away. Who are we without our occupations or vocations? Those supporting a person who has lost a job should be aware of this assault to self.

Our jobs form the structure of our days. In addition to providing a paycheck, work can bring meaning, challenge, order, and social structure to our lives. When a layoff, downsizing, or an outright firing occurs, we speak in terms of "losing a job." The phrase is accurate, as the loss is significant. And significant losses cause grief.

Factors involved in job loss can affect the grieving process. If the employee has a choice in the matter, the effects may be less than if no choice were involved. If the loss was anticipated, the effects can be less than if the loss were sudden. If a severance package and reemployment assistance is offered, the effects may be less than if the employee feels "out on the street." If the matter was handled with compassion and understanding, the effects are likely less than if the dynamics were insensitive.

Even under the best of circumstances, job loss can be devastating.

Even under the best of circumstances, though, job loss can be devastating. Job losses can cause victims to question their abilities, marketability, even their sense of self-worth. For people who have defined themselves by their jobs for any length of time, there can be a loss of identity. Loss of employment may bring with it other losses, such as loss of purpose, structure, social systems, financial resources, health and retirement benefits, and security.

Often the effects of these losses can cause the unemployed to want to isolate themselves. They may be embarrassed and ashamed and may not think that they want to talk about their losses. But isolation and bottling up the pain are not helpful in the grief process.

When someone isolates, the Dwarfs of Despair are most likely to take up residence. Spacey's usually there first—often completely dismayed and incredulous that job loss has occurred. Even if the loss has been expected, its finality can come as a shock. As soon as Spacey wanders off a bit, Angry usually roars onto the scene—letting anybody and everybody know the injustice of it all. When Angry stops the constant ranting, Empty comes in, recounting how all that hard work was for nothing. Further, Empty can make it difficult to envision a fulfilling future.

Meanwhile, Worry is pacing around the place, prattling on about how it's going to be impossible to make it, what with the bills, the mortgage, the car payments, the tuitions, the kids' activity fees, doctor bills, the TV that should never have been bought, the credit card debt, the lack of retirement funds, the probability of homelessness. When Worry shows up, he brings a trunk, planning to stay a long, long time, talking often about the griever's lack of skills and the unlikelihood of ever getting a job again. Not pleasant company for one who has lost a job.

What is pleasant company is a visit from a friend or family member who is willing to be present. When a supporter sits with a person in pain, empathetically listens, searches the way into this person's unique job loss experience, and receives the many emotions that emerge at a time of job loss, the griever can feel heard, understood, and validated. The supporter cannot change the situation but can change the experience for the one who lost the job by showing solidarity with the other along this desolate part of life's journey.

One area of caution for supporters in this situation of loss involves finances. Job loss can cause considerable stress over financial concerns. The unemployed's financial matters are personal and private, though they may be shared in regard to the effects of the job loss. It is good for supporters to attend to Loss Lesson #4—The Limitations of Support. Unless supporters can help with the job search, they cannot fix the job loss situation. If supporters think it is a good idea to contribute financially to alleviate the situation, they should remember that lending money or other material items of support could cause stress and strain on relationships. The stress can sometimes be minimized if any assistance is given in the form of a gift rather than a loan. In that fashion, there is no debt to be cleared or disputed. This matter should be seriously considered, though, because even gifts given with the best of intentions can create a sense of dependency or indebtedness that can diminish the mutuality in a relationship.

Many who have lost a job can later look back on the time as one that was defining and life-changing in a good way. The change forced decisions that may not have otherwise been faced. The rewards—in different career directions or changed priorities or a more leisurely pace of life or more family time—are later said to be well worth the pain of the transition. While it's good for supporters to understand this, they must be careful to respond to the person where he or she is and not present a glorified view of a future that will not ring true in the midst of pain and hopelessness. I recently tried to reassure someone who had lost her job, writing in the context of a long e-mail, "The cloud will lift." She responded with a curt, "The cloud is awful." By trying to instill hope, I wasn't sensitive to her emotional state at that moment. I have learned my lesson. A gentle, supportive presence can help the one who is grieving a job loss to find his or her way to hope.

from a woman who lost her job:

I felt like the biggest failure in the whole world when I found myself jobless, financially ruined, and without much in the way of prospects. I had never been out of work for more than a week before. To find myself as an adult with two children to raise on my own now scrambling to get a waitress job was mortifying. My whole identity was immersed in my job skills and my abilities to maintain a certain lifestyle. Losing my job and finding myself out of money changed my whole outlook on life.

Now, years later, after having gotten first a waitress job, then other kinds of jobs more related to my field, I realize that I am the best me I can be. No matter what happens in the future, I can't let my work define me. As long as I keep my priorities straight, nothing can daunt me. I don't allow my worth to be defined by my wallet anymore.

When others are going through job loss, mostly I just listen. I don't judge, and I give as much of myself as I can, because I've been there. I help with kids if it lifts the load; I give a shoulder or whatever is needed. I've found that it's best to follow whatever lead someone gives you when they're going through this, because often, that person won't want you to know the depth of their financial stress. It's such a private matter, and I respect that deeply.

The To-Be List in Chapter 4 contains actions and attitudes that are generally appropriate for many types of loss. Those included here are specifically helpful for the loss of employment.

support for job loss:

- Offer help getting or organizing information on unemployment benefits, insurance matters, etc.

- Offer to aid the job search process.

  - Offer to help explore resume-writing services and job search services.

  - Offer to watch children while the person does job search-related tasks.

  - Ask how others can network on the person's behalf in searching for a new job.

- Be careful to do what is useful, but not too much— the person has lost his or her job, but not his or her level of competence.

- If the person is lethargic, invite him or her to go on a walk or engage in another physical activity.

- Be careful about giving and loaning money.

  - Money matters can change relationships. Think through decisions and implications carefully and understand the relational risks in giving gifts or loans.

- Attend to the spouse, partner, and/or family
  of the one who has lost a job.

  - Realize that financial difficulties and
    changes in status can stress relationships.

  - Receive emotions expressed about the situation,
    but don't speak against the unemployed.

    - "You sound very angry."

    - "This is such a hard time."

    - "Life can be so unfair."

    - "I hear you."

Retirement

Some may see retirement in a book about loss and assume that
it's a joke or a mistake. Retirement, a loss?!? There are retirees
who have no trouble at all with retirement and embrace
it from day one. Often, if retirement has been anticipated
and planned for, the life change is readily celebrated.

For others, though, the transition may be more difficult.
Retirees may miss the work (especially if it was fulfilling),
the people, the structure, the physical surroundings,

the place to go each day that was someplace other
than home and, last but not least, the paycheck. The
transition is challenging enough if retirement is a choice.
If retirement was chosen for the worker, the transition
can be even more difficult.

An aspect of retirement that is not usually associated
with other forms of job loss can be a heightened sense
of mortality. Retirement traditionally is the beginning
of "the last stage of life." Some people see this phase
as a time to do what they have always wanted to do.
For others, though, retirement carries with it more of a
sense of loss—especially if the job provided significance,
meaning, and interest to life. For those who miss their jobs
and previous lifestyles, the Dwarfs of Despair, especially
Empty, Lonely, and Gloomy, may stop by for a chat and
end up overstaying their welcome.

Supporters can be helpful by listening to discover, rather
than assuming they already know, how the retiree
is experiencing this new phase of life. People who start
conversations with "I'm so jealous" or "must be nice"
or "of course, you don't have to worry about what we
workers have to deal with" close the door for retirees to express their possibly mixed feelings. Listening empathetically
goes a long way toward providing support, attention, and
care to retirees in all stages of what can be seen as
the end of one's working life.

from a recently retired woman:

Retirement emotions, for me, mirror those of many other transitions in my life. No matter how much I thought I had rationally planned for this new time in my life, I was left with lots of mixed feelings, all fighting it out in my brain. I was happy to have more personal time! I was sad to no longer see work friends. I was sad about losing a creative focus for my work. I was happy to have more time with my dear husband. I was sad to have to share the computer with him. You get the drift. One more quandary—what do I call myself now? I haven't come up with a great answer yet— now I'm just me. It helped to have coffee with friends who had retired already. One wise friend said that she'd decided to take a whole year after she retired before deciding what she was going to do next.

One quote I found has been especially helpful: "Want what you have." This told me that I didn't need new clothes, furniture, or fancy experiences. It made me focus on the beauty of my life now. I've tried to refocus on exercise and healthy cooking, with occasional chocolate and wine to savor.

I hope that I'm the same person I was before I retired—just without so much stress and multitasking distracting me from appreciating each day, each person, each season. This morning, I returned from my exercise class and watched a mockingbird sorting through the compost—mundane and magnificent, all at once.

from a recently retired man:

For me, retirement was not the leisurely pleasure that most people expect. There didn't seem to be any point to my days. My reason to get out of bed, take a shower, and get going was gone. I was bored. Aside from menial chores around the house, I had nothing to do. I was afraid I'd fall into the abyss of daytime TV.

Being able to talk candidly to people who had similar experiences helped a lot. A couple of friends who retired before I did independently invited me for lunch or a drink. I think they suspected from their own experiences that everything might not be sunshine and roses. They helped me realize that what I was feeling was normal and that the world is filled with worthwhile things to do.

People who enviously assumed that I must be in seventh heaven made me feel like a first-class failure when it comes to enjoying leisure. People who meant well but only mumbled platitudes like "Oh, sure, it takes some adjusting" or "You'll get used to it eventually" made me feel condemned to unfulfilling "golden years."

The To-Be List in Chapter 4 contains actions and attitudes that are generally appropriate for many types of loss. Those included here are specifically helpful for those who are uncomfortable with retirement.

support for the retired:

- Spend time with the retired—in person or by phone or e-mail.

- Ask questions about the person and his or her new lifestyle.

- Ask about the person's former work.

  - What aspect of work is missed most?

  - What about work is not at all missed?

  - What do you like most and least about your new lifestyle?

  - How has retirement changed your relationship with your spouse? Your children? Your friends and neighbors?

  - What in your days do you now look forward to?

  - What do you dread?

  - Are there new hobbies you'd now like to pursue?

  - What would it take to get you started in your new interests?

- Share your nonwork interests.

- Explore hobbies and activities you can do together.

- Feel free to discuss your workplace if the retiree
  is interested.

- Hear any emotions regarding challenges retirement
  may cause for the retiree's relationship with his
  or her spouse or significant other, but don't take
  sides or judge.

  - Respond with nonjudgmental comments like,
    "This is a time of transition" or "Change is hard."

- Suggest (or help put together) a memory book
  to detail work experience.

For those who can process and adjust to the changes that
retirement brings, this phase of life can bring rich rewards
as people can slow down and enjoy people and things that
really matter to them.

chapter eight

loss of

Health

Supporting Those Who Face Health Challenges

As I write this, I'm waiting by the phone to hear from my mom, who's waiting by her phone to hear from Helen, her best friend of 57 years. Helen has taken her husband, Jack, into the hospital for a brain scan and radiation. Two days ago, after a brief spell of confusion, he was taken to the doctor and subsequently diagnosed with brain cancer. Results of the scan will determine the course of Helen's and Jack's lives. And so we wait, and we pray—Helen and Jack, who are surrounded by family in their home, my mom across town from Helen, me across the country.

We wait and pray and hold Helen and Jack tenderly in our hearts, and we hope beyond all possible hope for good news.

Supporters of those who are dealing with health challenges can help by acknowledging the griever's experience of loss.

So many people live with the threat or reality of serious illness. As baby boomers become seniors, there will be more and more serious illnesses and greater and greater need for support. Living with disease means living with the losses that serious illness brings—loss of peace of mind, comfort, mobility, mental and physical abilities, independence, loss of the ability to participate in favorite activities, loss of the likelihood of a long and healthy future. Each loss is a little death, of sorts, as Loss Lesson #2—Little Deaths explains. Each loss can be grieved.

Supporters of those who are dealing with health challenges can help first by acknowledging the griever's experience of loss. Often, people try to cheer the griever up by looking at the bright side or by focusing on the good. They might say things like, "Don't worry about not being able to drive—now you get to be driven around like movie stars are" or "You're lucky not to be able to hear all this crazy conversation." Attempts to minimize the loss of any kind of functioning can dismiss the griever's feelings of loss. When loss is acknowledged and properly grieved, the person has a better chance of coming to terms with the loss. Supporters who listen empathetically to emotional expression regarding the effects of the loss are doing the griever a great service.

The loss does not have to have entirely negative consequences. It's helpful for supporters to know that health challenges and diminished functioning can bring about new possibilities. People diagnosed with illness sometimes feel an impetus to do things they have long put off. Many make the most of the times they feel good and rest during the bad days. Fractured relationships may be repaired, and good relationships may be made even stronger. Life may become even more precious, and often, more is made of every moment. Memories can take on new significance. Supporters can be present for these positive effects of diagnosis, as well as for the painful moments.

Often, when someone is suffering with major illness, there is a primary caregiver. Illnesses such as Alzheimer's are often long in duration, with the patient exhibiting greater and greater dependency needs as years go by. The level of care required by a caregiver can range from demanding to exhausting to overwhelming to impossible. Difficult decisions regarding patient care must be made—decisions with significant relational, emotional, and financial implications. Helping to support the primary caregiver is an important part of the process of providing support in situations of serious, long-term illness. Supporters can be present to the caregivers in the same way that it is helpful to support anyone who is grieving. Caregivers are most likely grieving all the "little deaths" in their loved ones' lives.

In the same way that every grief experience is unique, every illness is unique. The ways support can be offered are individual also. The support needed depends on the condition, the level of need, the availability of resources, the closeness of the relationship between supporter and the victim and the primary caregiver. In times of serious illness when losses of health and mobility are being mourned, the gift of a supporter's helpful and care-full presence is often deeply appreciated.

from a woman with MS:

When I was diagnosed with MS, oddly enough, I was somewhat relieved. Like most MS patients, I'd been having assorted strange symptoms for two years, made countless doctors' appointments, and had been through batteries of tests. One of my best friends had been diagnosed with MS a few years before, so I'd already read up on the illness and knew that while it was devastating, even fatal, to some patients, it was only an inconvenience to others. I chose to believe I'd be one of the lucky ones.

However, I also began to worry obsessively. I was most afraid that my quality of life or personality changes would hurt my marriage. The initial treatments made me jittery. I couldn't sleep. It took me about six months to get past thinking about my MS all the time. Luckily, it hasn't affected my world too much—just made me value life more and be more careful of my health. Fatigue is a given, but I try not to get too run down.

What helped me was feeling validated about my emotions and reactions. I made one visit to a psychologist, who assured me that my worries and tears were simply part of the normal grieving process and that nothing required professional intervention. It helped to hear from an outsider that I was a strong person. What was not helpful was people asking if I could manage a walk across a parking lot—that sort of thing. There were also a few dumb remarks like "I thought you were too old for MS." Mostly, though, I feel very lucky and appreciative of the amazing outpouring of love and support that comes my way. Now I'm more likely to send cards and cook for those who are sick or grieving, because those gestures meant so much to me.

The To-Be List in Chapter 4 contains actions and attitudes that are generally appropriate for many types of loss. Those included here are specifically helpful for the loss of health.

Supporting Victims of Health Loss

- Become educated about the illness.

  - Get information from relevant national organizations for the caregiver, if any, and for you to understand more about the sickness.

- Offer to help with things the ill person truly can't do anymore.

- Don't treat the person like a child.
  Respect present capabilities.

- Offer to spend time with the ill person.

  - Ask what times or days he or she likes
    to have company.

  - Offer to bring books or magazines. Ask if the
    ill person would like for you to read out loud
    or if he/she would like books on CD or tape.

  - Ask if there are any activities the two
    of you could do that would be enjoyable,
    such as playing cards.

  - If the ill person is in the hospital or a care
    center, offer to bring anything that would
    make the surroundings more comfortable.

  - If you live far away, ask if he or she would
    like to communicate by phone or e-mail.

  - Ask if there is anything you can do
    to make him or her more comfortable.

  - Let the ill person set the tone for conversation.

Suggestions **for talking with
someone with a serious illness:**

Instead of saying:	Say:
Don't be negative— you can beat this!	It must be difficult to come to terms with all this.
It doesn't matter that you can't drive anymore— you can get drivers!	What is it like to give up your driving independence?
This is too hard for me to hear.	I'm here for you and I'm strong. I'll listen to whatever you'd like to share.
I feel so helpless.	We are all here for you.
Don't give up! I can't do life without you!	I love you. If something were to happen, I would miss you terribly.
There has to be something more to do.	Let's be sure we get the best of medical treatments, and let's be together in doing all we can do.
Don't be down. You're sure to get well.	It must be hard. Can I just sit with you for a while?

if there is a primary caregiver, be attentive to his or her needs:

- Helpful things to say to a caregiver:

    - How are you doing?

    - What is hardest about caring for your loved one? What is most rewarding?

    - What would be helpful in terms of taking care of you?

    - What was life with your loved one like before the illness?

- Offer help to caregivers:

    - If Medicare and Medicaid are applicable, offer to help with understanding their rules and finding available facilities and services.

    - Suggest that the primary caregiver join a support group. Offer to help find available groups and times.

    - Offer to sit with the ill person to give the caregiver a break.

    - Help the caregiver set up a wide network of support.

- Help to investigate the kinds of support
  agencies offer.

- Offer to ask church, social, neighborhood,
  and organization-related groups about support
  services they can provide.

- Send cards or notes following updates
  and on important occasions, like
  major doctor appointments, treatments,
  improvements, or declines.

One of the greatest gifts a supporter can give to someone who is facing a serious illness or to a primary caregiver is the willingness to see the situation for what it is. The victim and the caregiver do not need cheerleaders who will try to make the situation seem better and thereby minimize the situation and the losses. In the same way, they do not need "supporters" who minimize the abilities of the afflicted and treat him or her like a dependent child. Supporters who are open and unflinchingly receptive to the realities of life lived with illness offer a safe emotional space for the grieving to be heard, validated, and accepted in all they are going through.

material
Loss

Supporting Those Who Have Lost Objects, Property, or Finances

In an instant, everything can change.
A thief can break into a house, apartment,
or car and take valued possessions. A fire
can destroy that which took a lifetime
to build and collect. A hurricane or tornado
can turn a warm family home into a heap
of destruction. A decision, a shift in the stock
market, or a bad run of luck can suddenly
change one's financial status.

Loss of Objects

When people experience losses of property or significant objects, grief is a natural response. It is natural for people to form attachments to things that have meaning to them. When the object or property disappears or is destroyed, the attachment is severed.

Material possessions and properties can be important for two reasons. Things can have intrinsic meaning, in that their worth is inherent in the objects or properties. A piece of jewelry might be loved for its delicate and intricate qualities. A home might be loved for its simple style and lake-view balconies. Or things can be valued because of their extrinsic value, in that their meaning and significance come from something beyond the object or property itself. They are loved, in part, because of what they represent. A ring can be treasured because it was your great-grandmother's. A cottage has been in the family for generations, and every summer, grandmas and grandpas, aunts, uncles, cousins, siblings, and spouses gather for leisurely time together. Of course, things can have both intrinsic and extrinsic value. The loss of objects and properties with extrinsic value are often the more difficult to weather.

Material loss can be caused by many things, one of them being theft. Theft is always shocking, always unexpected. With a theft can come a loss of trust, a loss of the sense of security, and a loss of innocence. After a theft, people often feel shaken, violated, and much more fearful.

The Dwarfs of Despair are quick to break and enter. Spacey can show up initially and then keep making repeat visits, as the magnitude and implications of the loss are processed. Angry is usually a chief resident. Victims are often furious at the audacity of thieves barging into the victims' lives and taking what is not theirs. Additionally, there can be anger at the time, expense, and hassle of replacing what was stolen. Some things can be replaced; many things can never be replaced—especially those things of extrinsic value. The Worry dwarf usually has a field day after losses caused by theft. People and situations that were never before deemed as suspicious can become so when the trust threshold has been lowered.

Empty and Gloomy can also make repeated showings after a theft. Every time the victim turns to use or enjoy whatever is missing, he or she is again reminded of the crime and the resulting absence of the object.

from the victim of a burglary:

When someone broke into my car and stole my purse and briefcase (which contained my work laptop), I felt many things. Initially, I was shocked, like "Is this really happening" because I have never experienced anything like this. Then I was scared and just wanted to get away from the crime scene as quickly as possible. Then as I was driving home,

I was sick to my stomach and bawling all the way (not to mention freezing since it was winter and my window was broken out). Then I felt guilty, like it was my fault that I left my purse in the car—although not in plain view as it was hidden under the back seat—(which had tinted windows). I thought my husband was going to be very upset with me for doing something so stupid. Then I was mad at the criminal, who felt it was his right to take my personal things instead of earning an honest living!

In the weeks following the crime, I really felt violated more than anything else as I kept remembering personal items that were in my purse that I could never get back and were now in a stranger's hands. This stranger had my Palm Pilot with all of my personal passwords and those of some of family members (like entry codes to their security systems). Very scary!

What was helpful? First, my husband was awesome. He immediately wanted to make sure I was OK before even asking about what was taken or if the car was OK. He then helped me start calling all the credit card companies, since I could barely function that night. At work, I really appreciated all of the concern people expressed and offers to help with anything I might need. Since my parking pass to the garage was in my briefcase, one of my co-workers lent me hers that she wasn't using. Other people offered to print out my online calendar, since I had no laptop. Many people stopped by to say how sorry they were, and it was just nice to know people cared.

What was not helpful? A few people immediately jumped to my stupidity of leaving those valuable things in the car, which just made me feel less like a victim and more like an idiot. They went on to point out that cars are broken in to every day downtown and I was nothing special. Even though I think they were trying to just make light of the situation, I found it very frustrating, since it didn't feel at all light to me.

Objects can be lost for reasons other than theft. Things break. Things wear out. Things just plain get lost. Carelessness happens. When a loss happens because of a person's carelessness or neglect, often the Guilty dwarf shows up with his incessant "You could've..." "You should've..." "Why didn't ya..." talk. Guilty can make significant losses quite hard to bear. Often, even when the loss is unexplainable, people who have lost important objects become self-incriminating, thinking there is *something* they could have done to prevent this painful loss. Assigning blame is not helpful in the grieving process.

Supporters can help those who are grieving by letting them name the loss and express all the emotions that the loss provokes. Attempts to minimize the loss are not helpful. Yes, it is good that the person was not hurt, but the victim may not want to look for the good in a situation that is, at the moment, pretty awful. Any talk of the loss being "just things" impedes the grieving process—such an approach can make the victim feel overly materialistic or feel like priorities are misguided. A victim has every right to be angry when such an injustice occurs. A victim has every right to grieve the profound loss of a significant object. A helpful supporter will be receptive to all expressions of emotion regarding the loss.

from a woman who lost an heirloom:

The moment I realized I didn't have my grandma's antique diamond engagement ring on my finger, my heart sank to my shoes. In an instant, I was tearing through the mall, down the stairs to the restroom, opening the heavy metal door, dashing to the third sink on the right. "Ohmygod-OhmygodOhmygod," I said as I realized the ring was no-where to be seen on the sink where I was sure I had left it. I got down on my hands and knees on that dirty linoleum floor, crawling around pipes, nose four inches from the floor in hopes of finding it. Nowhere. Why, oh why had I taken it off? I'd been eating caramel corn and wanted to get the stickiness off my hands…then the close-by towel machine didn't work, so I went across the restroom…my cell phone rang…it was my son, who needed a ride (was he safe?), and I forgot. I walked out drying my hands, talking to my son, forgetting my ring. I spent hours with Mall Security, I posted reward posters, I went back to that damned bathroom day after day, and no ring. I can't tell you how devastated I am not to have that ring—the only thing I have of my favorite grandmother, who died seven years ago on my birthday. I can't tell you how furious I was at my own stupidity. I went to her gravesite and cried and cried, telling Grandma how very sorry I was.

One friend, Carol, understood my loss. I called her the night I lost the ring—at midnight. She listened to me cry. She listened to my anger at myself. She listened to me cry some more. I don't remember her saying anything more than, "Oh, sweetie." "Oh, honey." "I'm so sorry." She never, ever mentioned the fact that it was my fault. Man, she's good. She still lets me go on about that ring. And she listens every time. And every time, she gives me an "Oh, honey," just when I need it most. If I had to lose that ring, I'm just glad I have my friend.

Loss of Property

Loss of property can occur in a variety of ways. Fires, hurricanes, floods, tornadoes, landslides…unfortunately, the list goes on and on. Most of the time, these disaster-related causes are sudden, with varying degrees of warning. Always, the losses are difficult because of their many effects on victims. People's houses are more than dwelling places; they are supposed to be havens of comfort, security, safety, and love. When the dwelling is damaged or destroyed, all that the haven has meant is, for the time being, no more. There is much to grieve.

Throughout the process of grieving, all of the Dwarfs of Despair are likely to visit. Especially in cases of disaster, Spacey is likely to show up. It can be so hard to believe that the home that was perfectly sound and normal at breakfast time was burned down before dinner. When the victims view the damage of their beloved home, either the Angry or the Gloomy dwarf—or both—shows up, bringing fury and/or deep despair. Guilty can do a quick drive-by to question whether or not anything could have been done to prevent this. Worry usually moves in for the duration, going on about replacement costs, insurance quagmires, changes in lifestyle, and the victims' well-being.

from a daughter of tornado victims:

On May 4, 2003, an F-4 tornado dropped out of the sky directly onto my elderly parents' patio home. Luckily, they weren't hurt—for once, they had listened to me and had gone to the basement just in time—but their neighborhood was devastated. I had been looking after my parents for years, but I didn't know very much about how to handle the immediate aftermath of that kind of damage.

I have two friends I don't mind calling "pushy." I call them that to their faces. They're proud of it. I learned to appreciate these "pushy" people when a real disaster happened. A lot of people, upon hearing about the tornado, immediately tried to top this tornado with stories of stronger tornadoes (F5s) they'd known of. A lot of people offered sympathy but didn't know any more than I did about the practical things to do in the aftereffects of this disaster. Only two people immediately said, "Is there anything I can do?" You guessed it—my two "pushy" friends. First, they figured out what needed to be done, and then they helped to get it done. My parents and I are forever grateful that they showed up and helped to do whatever it took to help my parents put their lives back together again.

Loss of property can occur for reasons other than disaster. Often a move can be experienced as a loss. Many times, a move from one property to another is a good and exciting adventure. But other times, the move is a necessary circumstance, causing a feeling of loss. Sometimes people must move from a beloved home to a less expensive place for financial reasons. Sometimes an older person must move from a family home to an assisted living facility. Sometimes a company transfer causes a family to move from a place of residence close to beloved family and friends to a strange new environment several time zones away from loved ones.

Often in a move that is not chosen, the Dwarfs of Despair jump right on the moving truck. Spacey is first on board. A move is hard enough when the move is desired—there are boxes to pack, utilities to turn off and turn on, addresses to change, cleaning and sorting to do. The list seems endless.

The tasks can be much more daunting when the move is less than desired. Spacey can hang around for a long time, talking the mover into avoiding all that needs to be done. Angry can be present but is sometimes relegated to the basement, as anger is not often allowed appropriate expression. For instance, family members often tell older people expressing anger at needing to move from their home, "Now, we've discussed this, and you know that it's for the best for all of us." If reluctant movers feel that they cannot acknowledge their true anger, the grief process can be impeded. The Lonely and Empty dwarfs are the first in the new residences—talking endlessly about life in the place left behind, bemoaning the lack of familiarity in the new place. Guilty may show up, berating the reluctant mover for having so many negative feelings. Worry prattles on that nothing will ever get better. And Gloomy starts unpacking endless baggage, making it known that he is here to stay. Not a great moving crew.

The best supporters are there for the duration.

When supporters show up (in person or by e-mail, phone calls, or through cards), the Dwarfs of Despair can quickly feel uninvited. Supporters can help assess an appropriate response depending on the nature of their relationships with grievers. Supporters can often help those who have suffered in material ways. They can open up their homes, closets, hearts, and souls and give whatever is needed to provide short-term and long-term help. And lastly, supporters can help victims rebuild new lives in either the renovated spaces or in entirely new places.

A caution: Before giving material or financial help after loss, consider the effects it may have on the relationship. Often a gift instead of a loan creates less stress in the relationship. But even a gift can create a sense of dependency or obligation on the victim's part. And gifts or loans can diminish the quality of mutuality in the relationship. The supporter must assess what is appropriate to the situation and to the relationship. The supporter and the victim can even talk about the implications of the gift or loan together, determining a solution that seems comfortable to both. Before making a gift or loan, supporters do well to consider all the implications, possibly even consulting a counselor, clergyperson, or other professional for advice.

Renovation or relocating after loss due to disaster or to a move requires continued support through the long process of reestablishing the sense of "home." The best supporters are there for the duration.

from a woman who is reluctant to move:

I love my home. I've lived here for 53 years, raised four children here—my husband and I did—before he died seventeen years ago. I've got a daughter here in town, two on the West

Coast, and a son in Georgia. They all think it's time for me to go to a senior living community, and I guess they're right. At least they won't worry about me as much. My niece is going to buy this house, and I'm glad for her. She says she loves it. I guess it's time for me to go. But I don't want to go. I can't even think about it right now.

When the property that is lost is a residence, the loss is very public. There is a new address, often a new phone number. There is the moving or renovating process. Consequently, there are many opportunities for supporters to reach out and offer care—such as helping to move, bringing or sending housewarming gifts, sending cards to the new address or cards to celebrate a restored home. There are other material losses that are not as public and, therefore, do not offer ready opportunities for supporters to extend care.

financial loss

This is one kind of loss no one likes to talk about. Certainly, the victims of financial loss are not quick to broadcast it. Those wanting to be supportive may feel awkward and intrusive addressing this loss, as finances are, indeed, a personal and private matter. Still, we know that financial losses happen, and when they do, they can be disruptive at best, devastating at worst. If victims of financial losses feel completely alone, unable to receive support, the grieving process can be more difficult.

Financial losses can occur for a variety of reasons. Job loss, already discussed in Chapter 7, is one. Investment loss is another. Some people, like Enron employees, lost most if not all of their retirement accounts because of corporate mismanagement. Real estate factors, such as depreciation or subprime mortgage lending fiascos, can cause financial losses. Divorce, legal, employment, medical, credit, and addiction-related issues can all result in financial losses.

When financial loss occurs, two Dwarfs of Despair often play tag team. Spacey often shows up saying things aren't so bad and suggests a quick fix that can make things all better. (Spacey is so dim that he actually thinks these schemes can work.) The other player is the Guilty dwarf, who is heavily into incrimination and blame.

The other dwarfs, Empty, Lonely, Angry, Worry, and Gloomy, will eventually join Spacey and Guilty. With financial loss, the dwarfs aren't the only unwelcome intruders. They often bring the giant of Shame along with them. For this reason, financial loss is often the loss most grieved in isolation.

Supporters can help to end the victim's isolation. If a supporter senses that there is something amiss, he or she can help by initiating contact with the victim. When the supporter and the victim connect, it is helpful for the supporter to create an emotionally safe space for the victim to open up about anything he or she wants to talk about. Creating an emotionally safe space is often about being with the victim on the victim's terms. If the victim wants to talk about the loss, supporters can listen empathetically, without judgment or condemnation. Even if the financial loss is not discussed at all, the supporter's presence (in person, by phone or e-mail) can be beneficial by helping to normalize the victim's world and helping him or her to not feel so alone.

The victim may immediately open up about the cause of the grief or may do so after some time. Such information should not be forced. Open-ended questions such as "How are you doing?" or "How is everything?" can open up the space for the victim to share if sharing is desired. If the victim does disclose information about the loss, the supporter will do well to remember Loss Lesson #4—the Limitations of Loss Support. The supporter's role is not to fix the situation but to be present to the person in his or her loss and pain. If the victim shows signs of self-blame, self-incrimination, remorse, and regret, the supporter can be helpful by being receptive to—hearing, taking in, understanding—all of these feelings. The supporter's response can be helpful if it is an honest and genuine expression of how the victim's words are affecting him or her.

Honest, genuine responses, such as those suggested in the list at the end of this chapter, enable the supporter to communicate sincere support and solidarity even when the victim is at fault for what happened. Attempts to absolve the person of his or her guilt usually don't work, because the most powerful forgiveness will come from the victim's family and from himself or herself. However, a supporter's gentle, empathetic, responsive, nonjudgmental presence can set the stage for self-forgiveness to occur.

from a man who suffered financial loss:

I got hammered twice in speculative stock busts. The losses did not take me from luxury to hardship, even though they were quite significant. I could and can still live a comfortable life, but the losses required some adjustment to future plans and worldview. Aside from a lot of money just being gone in a flash, the worst things were that I felt like a fool, a real slow learner, and that I felt swindled, like I could never again trust in things as I once had.

supporting those who have lost property or finances:

- Offer support immediately after hearing of the loss and on an ongoing nature.

- Offer to help the victims of disaster research support agencies.

- Offer to help victims of crime with police matters.

- Offer to help with replacement issues—prioritizing tasks, keeping records, dealing with insurance agents, shopping for replacements.

- Offer to help set up a support system among friends and relatives.

- Think carefully before giving or loaning money.

  - A gift may create less relational stress than a loan, but gifts can damage mutuality and create a sense of dependency and obligation.

- Do say:

  - "I feel really sad to hear of your loss."

  - "I understand everything you said about the circumstances that led you to that decision."

  - "I hear how painful this is for you."

  - "I am inspired by all you have learned through this."

  - "I am deeply touched by your concern for your family and your wanting to make this right."

- Do not minimize the loss.

- Do not say:

  - "At least nobody got hurt."

- "It was God's will."

- "Good things will come."

- "It's not that bad" or "It could be worse."

- Keep checking on the person/family long after the event happened.

Even though material things and property can be replaced, often the new things or places do not hold the emotional significance of the ones that were destroyed. Supporters who are sensitive to the possible ongoing nature of material loss can most effectively aid the grieving process by helping the grievers feel validated in their feelings and supported in their loss.

chapter ten

on a

Supportive Note

Supporting People Throughout Their Grief Processes

People care. They want to help. When significant loss happens, people want to express support and concern. Immediately after the loss is the customary time for people to do so. This is when visitations and funerals are held, when church groups and neighbors and co-workers set up casserole brigades, when cards fill the mailbox and flowers grace the mantel. Immediately after a divorce, friends invite the newly single woman to lunch. Immediately after a tornado, people arrive with bottled water and boxes of snacks. But after a few weeks, the casseroles and cards and expressions of care stop coming. The flowers die. People move on with their busy lives.

The truth is that after the initial phase of the loss is when people need support the most. In the initial phase, when all the support brigades are in full force, the Spacey dwarf is still keeping close company with the griever. Denial, distraction, confusion, lack of focus, and often the flurry of support-related activity can make the griever feel a sense of numbness. It's when the activity subsides and the numbness gives way to the cold, stark reality of a life to be lived in context of profound loss that support is really needed. The lists in Chapter 4 offer many ways to provide ongoing support. Included in those lists are suggestions to occasionally send cards and notes. In this chapter, I offer specific ideas and examples for writing notes and cards.

The truth is that people most need support after the initial phase of a loss.

Notes and cards are wonderful ways to show ongoing support to grievers. They keep the lines of supportive communication open and can be read and reread at the griever's convenience. In our mobile society, cards offer ways for those who are in close or distant proximity to connect and communicate ongoing care and concern. In this age of instant messaging and e-mail, though, handwriting a note—especially about sensitive topics—is becoming a lost art. Notes and cards that tell the griever "I'm thinking of you" are in and of themselves a simple but effective means of support to those who have suffered loss—recently or in the past.

Handwritten notes matter, especially in times of loss. One woman who had recently lost her husband braced herself to face her first Valentine's Day without her beloved partner. As she contemplated how she would spend the evening, the widow prepared to be sad—to spend the whole night with the Gloomy dwarf. But then she got an idea. She made herself a nice dinner of her and her husband's favorite foods. Then she got out the shoebox in which she had saved all the cards her friends and family had sent since the death of her husband. While she ate, she pulled out the cards, one by one, and read the words inside. Many of her friends and family had written memories of her husband. All had expressed their love and care for her. She later said that for that Valentine's Day dinner, she felt completely surrounded by love—not only the love she and her husband shared but by the love of her family and friends who had supported her so beautifully since his death. Cards and notes matter.

Writing notes is really very simple—it's all about communicating, connecting, and caring. When you're doing those three things, you can't go wrong. To make it even easier, though, I'm offering some note templates for specific situations. Feel free to use these templates and alter them according to your own personality, your relationship with the griever, the situation of loss, and the time that has passed since the loss.

Writing Notes to Offer Ongoing Support

note-writing basics:

- Be warm.

- Be sincere.

- Be you.

Not all of these sending occasions are appropriate for all losses. The severity of the loss as well as the closeness of the card sender's relationship with the recipient is a determining factor. The greater the loss and the closer the relationship, the more frequently sending cards or notes is appropriate.

reasons to send a card or note:

- When you first hear of the loss, even if the loss happened a while back.

- Regularly after the loss at intervals that feel right for you and the recipient.

- The birthday of the griever.

- The birthday of the deceased.

- The anniversary of the death or event.

- The wedding anniversary if the loss is a divorce.

- Appropriate and significant holidays, for example:

  - New Year's Day

  - Valentine's Day

  - Easter

  - Mother's Day

  - Father's Day

  - 4th of July—if this was special
    to the couple/family

  - Thanksgiving

  - Christmas

  - Hanukkah

For further information and encouragement on note writing, see another Hallmark book, *On a Personal Note,* written by Angela Ensminger and Keely Chace.

Examples of notes **that can be written in greeting cards or on blank cards or stationery:**

loss of loved one—initial:

Dear Barb,

I'm still in shock that your dear brother, Paul, has died. I am so very sorry. I remember how much he loved the outdoors, how much life he brought to every person he met. Know that I'm keeping your family in my heart and in my prayers.

With deepest sympathy,

Peggy

loss of loved one—ongoing:

Dear Barb,

Here it is, one year after the death of Paul. I have been thinking of him so much and thinking about your love for him. I have been so enriched by your stories of him. I know this is a tender time for you. Know I'm thinking of you and will look forward to the next time we get together. I'd love to hear more stories about Paul.

Take care,

Peggy

loss of parent—initial:

Dear Bill,

I want to express my sympathy over the loss of your father. Know that you are surrounded by people who care about you and who grieve your loss.

Sincerely,

Carol

loss of parent—ongoing:

Dear Bill,

As Father's Day approaches, I can't help but think about you and the recent death of your dad. Just wanted you to know that I'm keeping you in my thoughts and that I remain so sorry for your loss.

Sincerely,

Carol

pregnancy loss—initial:

Dear Becky,

My heart went out to you when I heard of your miscarriage.

I want to express my deepest sympathy for your profound and tender loss. Know I will keep you and your family in my prayers.

I heard that your mother is in town now. I'll call at the end of the week to see how you are and to see if Kylie can come over to play. In the meantime, know I am here for you.

Love,

Susan

pregnancy loss—ongoing:

Dear Becky,

Here we are, close to what was supposed to be your due date. I just wanted to write you a note to let you know I'm thinking of you so much, especially at this time. Know you're not alone in your loss. I'm here for you.

With love,

Susan

loss of child—initial:

Dear Bob and Cindy,

Sam and I are so very sorry about the loss of Katie. She was such a smart, generous, creative young woman who faced her illness with strength and courage. Her positive spirit will continue to be an inspiration to us. She had a light about her that will live on in the hearts of all who knew her. Our deepest sympathy goes out to you. Know you will remain in our thoughts and prayers.

Sincerely,

Mary

loss of child—ongoing:

Dear Bob and Cindy,

I just wanted to write you a note as Katie's birthday approaches. I can only imagine how difficult this time must be. Know that her beautiful spirit lives on in our household. Stories about her grace, strength, and perseverance through the hardest times continue to be told around our dinner table. You gave the world a great gift with Katie.

Take care,

Mary

loss of spouse—initial:

Dear George,

I wanted to write to express my deepest sympathy for Barbara's death. As you know, I lost Lois almost a year ago. Though our experiences aren't the same, I have some idea of what you might be going through. Know I'm thinking of you and am glad to help if you need anything. I'll call next week and see if you want to get dinner.

With sympathy,

Fred

loss of spouse—ongoing:

Dear George,

It's springtime and I can't help but think of Barbara. How she loved flowers! I always walked by your yard so that I could see her budding jonquils and daffodils. She added such beauty to life in so many ways. And how she loved you! I hope you're still feeling her love and embracing her beautiful memory. I'd love to share my favorite Barbara stories, if you'd like. I'll call this weekend and see if we can meet for coffee or something.

Take care,

Donna

loss of spouse from illness—initial:

Dear Fran,

I am so sorry to hear that John has died. I know that this has been such a long ordeal. You have shown such love and care throughout John's illness. I'll never forget the way he smiled that special smile when he talked about how much he loved and appreciated you. Know that I am holding you in my heart. I'll call in the next day or so to see how you are. Please call before then if there is any way I can be supportive.

Love,

Joan

loss of spouse from illness—ongoing:

Dear Fran,

I can't help but think of John during this, the week of his birthday. I remember how he always wanted to surround himself with family and friends to celebrate. He sure lived life to the fullest, didn't he? I have such wonderful memories of his croquet parties and all the laughter he brought. This week, especially, I'm thinking of him, thinking of you. I was wondering if you'd like to get together to look at some of the pictures we took of those parties? I'd love to reminisce about John and talk over old times if that feels right to you. I'll call later this week, and we can talk about getting together—with or without pictures. In the meantime, know you're in my thoughts.

Love,

Joan

loss of pet—initial:

Dear Sandy, Pete, Matt, Lucy, and Carrie,

Our family is so sorry to hear that Bosco has died. Every time we saw one of you taking him on a walk (which was all the time!), it made us smile. Bosco was always so full of life, so happy. Seeing how much you all enjoyed him made us happy. Know we will keep all of you in our thoughts at this very sad time.

With sympathy,

Katie (Carl, and Kimmy, too)

loss of pet—ongoing:

Dear Lucy,

Happy Birthday! How does it feel to be seven? I wish Bosco were here to celebrate. I'm sure he'd be chewing his bone in your honor. Hope you get every single present you want!

Have fun!

Katie, Carl, and Kimmy

loss of relationship—initial:

Dear Jim,

Mark and I heard from your brother that you and Marge are divorcing. We want you to know that we are here for you and the boys in whatever ways you need us. I'll be making a huge chocolate cake that I'll bring over this weekend. I'll call on Friday to see how you're doing and if there's anything else I can bring.

Take care,

Betty

Dear Marge,

Mark and I heard from Jim's brother that the two of you are divorcing. Our hearts go out to you and the boys. We want you to know that we're here for you and that we want to help in any way. I'll call in the next few days to see when you have the boys and if I could bring over some pizzas. In the meantime, call if you need anything at all.

Take care,

Betty

loss of relationship—ongoing:

Dear Jim,

I hear you're getting tons of snow up in the Northeast. I'll resist gloating over the weather down here. Hey, I just

wanted to touch base and see how you're doing. When I
went through my divorce, I remember the holidays the first
year as being rough. Just wanted you to know I'm thinking
of you, big brother. Call anytime. I'll call on Turkey Day
morning. Looking forward to seeing you at Christmas.

Best,

Jerry

loss of employment—initial:

Dear Sherry,

When I got your e-mail about your job being eliminated,
I was stunned. I know how dedicated you have been
to your job and how hard you have been working. I am
so very sorry for your loss. I will call in the next day
or so to see what you need and how I can help. In the
meantime, know you are surrounded by friends who
care so much about you.

With love,

Robin

loss of employment—ongoing:

Dear Sherry,

I just wanted you to know I'm thinking of you. I can only imagine what the job search must involve. Know I'm on hand with wine and chocolate. Put me on speed dial and I'll be there, popping the cork and unwrapping the truffles.

Always in your corner,

Robin

retirement—initial:

Dear Judy,

I just read in the newsletter that you have retired after 27 years of service. I can't imagine all the contributions you have made to the company in that time! I only know how well you are respected and how much you will be missed. I imagine retirement will be a change. I look forward to hearing about the transition. I'll give you time to get a little bit adjusted, and then I'll give you a call to see if we can set up a time for lunch. Call or e-mail if you want to connect before then. Until we talk, know you're in my best thoughts.

Warmly,

Jo Anne

retirement-ongoing:

Dear Judy,

I so enjoyed getting together with you last month and hearing about the weaving class you are taking. You've inspired me to take an art class—Watercolor 101! I just wanted to let you know that the way you are using retirement to pursue hobbies has encouraged me to take some risks, and I'm experiencing the creative rewards. I'll call in the next week or so to see if we can schedule another time to get together.

Take care,

Jo Anne

loss of health—initial:

Dear Mr. and Mrs. Brannigan,

I heard from my mom that Mr. Brannigan is going through some medical tests. I just wanted you both to know that I'm keeping you in my most heartfelt prayers, praying for the best possible results and for peace in the waiting. I have such fond memories of the two of you being present for so many important times throughout my family's life.

Know how much my whole family is sending love and support at this time.

Take good care,

Lee

loss of health—ongoing:

Dear Mr. and Mrs. Brannigan,

I just wanted to let you know that I'm keeping Mr. Brannigan in my prayers during this time of radiation treatment. I've always admired your marriage—how supportive you have been of each other for, what, over fifty years? I hope your love and deep care are sustaining you through this time of treatment. I'll be visiting Mom and Dad next month. I'll call when I get to town and see if there would be a good time to visit. In the meantime, know that you are being surrounded by support.

Take good care,

Lee

loss of property—initial:

Dear Steve and Jan,

I just heard that your house was damaged in the recent tornado. I can't imagine what you must be going through. I just wanted to write to let you know that you both are in my thoughts. If there's anything I can do or if there is anything you need, please let me know. I'll be calling to see how I can help. Again, I'm so sorry to hear about your loss.

Sincerely,

Lynne

loss of property—ongoing:

Dear Steve and Jan,

I'm so happy you've been able to rebuild your house. It sounds wonderful. Still, I'm sure there are special memories about your "old" house. Next time we're together, I'd love to hear the long version of what's the same, what's different. I'd especially like to see pictures if you'd like to show and tell! I'll call next week.

All the best,

Lynne

showing up...appropriately

The main message of this book is that reaching out to others in times of loss is 90 percent about showing up. Showing up appropriately. Showing up to be responsive to what others need. Showing up to be receptive to any and all emotions being expressed. Showing up to invite memories and, eventually, invite grievers into renewed participation in life. The main objective of this book is to better equip people to do just that.

Reaching out is about offering support again and again, all along the grief journey. It's not about avoiding the person so as to avoid the reality that loss happens. It's not about avoiding the person so as to avoid your own feelings of inadequacy in the situation. It's not about ignoring the loss so as to not remind the person of the loss. (Believe me, the griever does not need reminding. The loss is always there.) It's not about avoiding the person because life is too busy. It's not about taking away the pain.

Reaching out to others during times of loss is about being with them through the pain. It's about accompanying them on their journeys of grief, knowing that eventually, in their own time, in their own ways, they will get to the other side and once again reattach to other people and situations and things.

The word *accompany* comes from the Latin *panis*, which means bread. To accompany those who are grieving is like giving bread for the journey.

My hope is that this book will inspire and equip you to walk alongside others with your nourishing presence as they travel their journeys of grief. The gift of your attentive care will mean more than you'll ever know.

Acknowledgments

Much of my understanding of grief and loss is informed by *All Our Losses, All Our Griefs: Resources for Pastoral Care* by Kenneth R. Mitchell and Herbert Anderson. I am indebted to Philip Culbertson's book, *Caring for God's People,* for the definition I used of empathetic listening.

Additionally, I am grateful to colleagues, friends, and acquaintances for the personal accounts of grief and loss that are incorporated in this book. I want to particularly thank my editor, Jeff Morgan, for the opportunity to work on this project and for his invaluable feedback and contributions along the way.

While there are many resources available on grief,
I have found the following to be particularly helpful:

A Grief Observed by C. S. Lewis, Faber and Faber, Limited, 1961.

All Our Losses, All Our Griefs: Resources for Pastoral Care by Kenneth R. Mitchell and Herbert Anderson, Westminster John Knox Press, 1983.

Caring for God's People: Counseling and Christian Wholeness (Integrating Spirituality Into Pastoral Counseling) by Philip Culbertson, Augsburg Fortress, 2000.

Grieving the Death of a Friend by Harold Ivan Smith, Augsburg Fortress, 1996.

How to Survive the Loss of a Love by Melba Colgrove, Ph.D., Harold H. Bloomfield, M.D., and Peter McWilliams, Prelude Press, 1976, 1991.

Necessary Losses: The Loves, Illusions, Dependencies, and Impossible Expectations That All of Us Have to Give Up in Order to Grow by Judith Viorst, Simon & Schuster, 1986.

On Death and Dying by Elisabeth Kubler-Ross, M.D., Macmillan Publishing Company, 1969.

Surviving: Coping with a Life Crisis by Dr. Bob Montgomery and Dr. Laurel Morris, Fisher Books, 1989.

Mourning Handbook: A Complete Guide for the Bereaved by Helen Fitzgerald, Simon & Schuster, 1994.

The Year of Magical Thinking by Joan Didion, Alfred A. Knopf, 2006.

When Children Grieve: For Adults to Help Children Deal with Death, Divorce, Pet Loss, Moving, and Other Losses by John W. James and Russell Friedman, HarperCollins Publishers, 2001.

If you have found this book to be helpful,

Hallmark would love to hear from you.

Please send your comments to:
BOOK FEEDBACK
2501 McGee, Mail Drop 215
Kansas City, MO 64108

Or e-mail us at
booknotes@hallmark.com